ENERGIZING
SUPERFOOD
JUICES AND
SMOOTHIES

ENERGIZING
SUPERFOOD
JUICES AND
SMOOTHIES

NUTRIENT-DENSE, SEASONAL RECIPES
TO JUMP-START YOUR HEALTH

SHAUNA R. MARTIN
FOUNDER OF Daily Greens Beverages

FOREWORD BY Mayim Bialik

ROCK
POINT

Inspiring | Educating | Creating | Entertaining

Brimming with creative inspiration, how-to projects, and useful information to enrich your everyday life, Quarto Knows is a favourite destination for those pursuing their interests and passions. Visit our site and dig deeper with our books into your area of interest: Quarto Creates, Quarto Cooks, Quarto Homes, Quarto Lives, Quarto Drives, Quarto Explores, Quarto Gifts, or Quarto Kids.

This edition published in 2019 by Rock Point, an imprint of The Quarto Group, 142 West 36th Street, 4th Floor, New York, NY 10018, USA T (212) 779-4972 F (212) 779-6058 www.QuartoKnows.com

First published in 2015 by Race Point Publishing, an imprint of The Quarto Group, 142 West 36th Street, 4th Floor, New York, NY 10018, USA

Rock Point titles are also available at discount for retail, wholesale, promotional and bulk purchase. For details, contact the Special Sales Manager by email at specialsales@quarto.com or by mail at The Quarto Group, Attn: Special Sales Manager, 100 Cummings Center Suite, 265D, Beverly, MA 01915, USA.

Publisher: Rage Kindelsperger
Creative Director: Laura Drew
Managing Editor: Cara Donaldson
Senior Editor: Erin Canning
Photography: Bill Milne
Cover and Interior design: Evelin Kasikov
Layout: Kim Winscher

ISBN: 978-1-63106-642-9

10 9 8 7 6 5 4 3 2 1

Library of Congress Cataloging-in-Publication Data

Names: Martin, Shauna R, author.
Title: Energizing superfood juices and smoothies : over 60 nutrient-dense,
    seasonal recipes to jump-start your health / Shauna R Martinn, creator
    of Daily Greens Beverages ; foreword Mayim Bialik.
Description: New York, NY, USA : Rock Point, 2019.
Identifiers: LCCN 2019028173 (print) | LCCN 2019028174 (ebook) | ISBN
    9781631066429 (hardcover) | ISBN 9780760366141 (ebook)
Subjects: LCSH: Smoothies (Beverages) | Fruit juices. | Vegetable juices. |
    LCGFT: Cookbooks.
Classification: LCC TP562 .M28 2019 (print) | LCC TP562 (ebook) | DDC
    641.8/75--dc23
LC record available at https://lccn.loc.gov/2019028173
LC ebook record available at https://lccn.loc.gov/2019028174

Previously published as *Daily Greens 4-Day Cleanse*

Printed in China

MIX
Paper from responsible sources
FSC® C008047

I dedicate this book to all the young breast cancer warriors out there. Live life like you mean it!

In memory of all the fallen cowgirls (young women who have lost their battle with breast cancer). You may be gone from this earth, but you will not be forgotten.

In honor of and in memoriam to my sisterhood of fellow breast cancer warriors, I percent of the royalties from this book will be donated to programs that provide support and services to young women battling breast cancer.

NEW YEAR

SPRING

SUMMER

FALL

Foreword[*]

In my almost forty years on the planet, I have seen many eating and dieting trends come and go. No fat, low fat, high protein, no carbohydrates, raw, only cauliflower soup. . . You name it, and people have tried it! However, what remains consistently recommended by every leading doctor of every persuasion is that we need to eat less processed foods, more fruits and vegetables, and more foods in their natural state. Period.

I have been vegan for almost seven years and had been vegetarian for twenty years before that. I ate pretty healthy, but I have a confession to make: Since becoming a mom almost ten years ago, I have gotten in the habit of grabbing a handful of chips or pretzels or cookies here and there. Well, the "here and there" had lodged itself literally here and there, mainly around my hips and belly. This Mama had accumulated a little bit too much "here and there" . . . here and there.

This past year, I heard about juicing as a way of life, and honestly, it sounded weird, even though it held the possibility of helping me get rid of my "here and there," among other benefits. When I heard about Daily Greens through their founder, Shauna, her story really inspired me. I could relate to her perspective as a young mom who wanted to improve my health and designed these juices from that desire, but her experience battling cancer was really what touched me. I felt empowered because of her dedication and her motivation not only for her health, but for the health of others.

I had some concerns about attempting a juice cleanse despite all of my optimistic posturing. Although I never considered myself to have an unhealthy relationship with food, as I prepared to start the cleanse, I started to feel a sense of panic and impending doom. I felt like food was being taken away from me forever (even though that makes no logical sense!). Thankfully, I was able to acknowledge that these kinds of fears and this kind of panic were things that I could cleanse as well.

To make a four-day-juice-cleanse-story short, the juices tasted good enough that I didn't feel like I was being punished by drinking them. I snacked on raw stuff throughout the day like fruits and veggies. I simply wasn't hungry or grumpy at all. I felt full of energy. Simple foods started tasting really good to me, and that hasn't gone away even months after I've finished the cleanse.

I felt so good after my four-day cleanse that I kept going. I ended up eating raw for nine whole days, with one or two juices a day. I lost weight off my hips and tummy and can fit into my old jeans again!

I took a chance and was inspired enough to commit to disciplining my eating for four days. It transformed my palate, made my body healthier, and put me back in control of my eating and my relationship with food.

If that's trendy, count me in.

—Mayim Bialik, 2015

[*] This foreword was written to accompany the original version of this book, *Daily Greens 4-Day Cleanse.*

Introduction

I vividly recall sitting on the floor of my shower with water and tears streaming down my face trying to figure it all out. I could not stop thinking . . . why? Why me? What did I do wrong? On July 28, 2004, my son's first birthday, I had been diagnosed with breast cancer at the age of thirty-three. And then, just a few weeks later, my younger sister was also diagnosed with breast cancer at thirty-one years old.

Happier periods of my life started flashing through my mind as I sat in that shower. I remembered racing with my younger sister through banana plantations by a house we lived in during a four-year stint in Puerto Rico. We were probably eight and ten years old at the time, and I recall running barefoot through the trees, stopping to pick a banana or an orange here and there. Sometimes we would gather mangoes and avocados to take back to our mother to serve with dinner. As I sat on my shower floor mourning the loss of my breasts, I tried hard to remember. Didn't I also recall plantation workers spraying down those banana trees with pesticides? Were those pesticides the reason why my sister and I came to have aggressive

breast cancer, mine having grown unchecked into stage II breast cancer while I breastfed my son for nine months?

I flashed-forward a number of years to my grandmother's garden in Arkansas. My sister and I spent many happy hours helping her plant and pick tomatoes, okra, cucumbers, and all kinds of other wonderful vegetables. Again, I strained to remember that pesticide she used to put on the vegetables to keep the bugs away. What was it called? Sevin dust? Weren't we told that we had to keep the cats away from it for fear of their ingesting it and dying from it? I remember Grandma hollering at us not to eat the vegetables until she had a chance to wash off the "poison," and even the Centers for Disease Control reported in a study that a single dose of 250 mg consumed by an adult male resulted in "moderate poisoning." Was this why we had breast cancer? Had we eaten fruits and vegetables covered in poisonous pesticides that later settled in our breast tissue to form cancer cells? Was that possible? I started thinking about our college days and the TV dinners

Shauna with her husband, Kirk, and son, Cooper.

heated with plastic wrap and consumed quickly while in the midst of cramming for exams. Was it all the chemicals in the processed food that we ate?

We had no family history of breast cancer until we were both simultaneously diagnosed with the disease—years before our doctors would normally start screening us for breast cancer. In fact, no one in our immediate family had ever had any type of cancer. I had been to at least a half-dozen doctors who really had no answer for the "why." Most agreed that it was probably somehow genetic, although they admitted they were stumped by the fact that both my sister and I had tested negative for the known genetic mutations for breast cancer. Most of the physicians that I saw just threw up their hands and said we would probably never know the cause. They confirmed that not enough information is known about the genetic predisposition to breast cancer and certainly not enough information is known about the environmental and food-supply factors that could potentially cause breast cancer.

One thing the doctors did all seem to agree upon was that our treatment plans should be the most aggressive available. Before all was said and done, we each underwent a year of mind-numbing chemotherapy, double mastectomies, and multiple surgeries to reconstruct our breasts. Due to my advanced breast cancer, all of my lymph nodes had to be removed from under one of my arms, leaving me with lymphedema (swelling caused by poor drainage of lymph fluid) in my left arm, hand, and torso, which I will have for the rest of my life. Then, after six years of hormone therapy, my team of doctors advised me that I should also remove my ovaries to eliminate the risk of more breast cancer or, even worse, ovarian cancer. So at the age of thirty-nine, I had both ovaries removed, putting my body into premature and permanent menopause. Prior to our breast cancer diagnosis, my sister and I were the pictures of health. We were raised as vegetarians by our military doctor father and our registered nurse mother, who are both very health conscious and taught us to eat right, exercise daily, and watch our weight. We have never been even remotely obese, smoked a cigarette, or touched a piece of red meat (all the supposed top risk factors for breast cancer). So again, I had to ask, why?

THE JOURNEY FOR ANSWERS

It has now been over nine years since that fateful day when my doctor told me I had breast cancer, and I finally know the answer to the "why?" I was meant to have breast cancer so that I would go on a journey in search of answers. That journey would not only change my life, but also allow me to educate others, to assist in the growing movement to change the way America thinks about food and diet. The first part of my journey for answers entailed reading everything I could get my hands on about the connection between food and disease, and in particular the connection between food and cancer. On my required reading list were *The China Study*, by Dr. T. Colin Campbell and Thomas M. Campbell II, and Michael Pollan's *The Omnivore's Dilemma* and *In Defense of Food*. I learned from Dr. Campbell that there was likely a connection between the foods I had consumed and my untimely breast cancer. Dr. Campbell's fifty-year study of rural populations in China provides evidence of a direct connection between not only the consumption of animal products and cancer, but also between the overconsumption of animal

Sisters Tamara and Shauna.

products and a host of modern diseases currently plaguing the Western world, including heart disease, obesity, and autoimmune diseases.

From Michael Pollan, I learned the history of how we have applied the principles of Ford's mass production of cars to the mass production of food, which led to McDonald's and the proliferation of fast food in the US. Mr. Pollan educated me on the compromises made in the growing of food and the raising of animals in order to satiate the world's ever-growing demand for fast and processed foods—these compromises include the proliferation of genetically altered versions of our most consumed crops and animals, along with the introduction of pesticides and antibiotics to our food sources and onto our dinner plates. I realized that much of what I had been putting into my body for the first thirty-three years of my life was likely laden with pesticides or packaged with numerous chemical preservatives to create years of shelf life. I had been eating a diet that, while healthy by the measuring stick of the Food and Drug Administration and other government standards, was

possibly a contributing factor to my breast cancer.

I gained further inspiration from Kris Carr and her *Crazy Sexy Cancer* movie and books, which chronicle her journey from an incurable cancer into remission through her consumption of a raw, plant-based diet. I realized, with hope, that there might be some explanations as to why cancer had started to grow in my young body. While I was vegetarian for the most part, I overconsumed dairy products and processed foods. We are the only mammal that consumes the milk of another mammal, and as it turns out, our bodies do not process it very well. Dr. Campbell's studies showed a link between overconsumption of cow's milk products and cancer.

I will never forget the first time I got my hands on Kris Carr's first book, *Crazy Sexy Cancer Tips*, which included a short but powerful chapter on food. It contained an overview of her diet recommendations, and there was a picture that jumped out at me from the page: It showed the first and, at the time, only juice bar in Austin, and the establishment's sign read simply:

"Disease Can't Fight Oxygen and Light." Tears streamed down my face as I realized that I may have finally found something in my own crazy breast cancer journey that was under my control. I did not choose breast cancer, nor would I have chosen to remove my breasts and ultimately my ovaries in my thirties. But when you have a small child and a loving husband, you do whatever it takes to stay alive for them. You do what your doctors tell you to do, even if that means poisoning your body with toxic chemotherapy and removing all the offending body parts that harbor cancer. Finally, I had found something that was completely under my control and within my power. From my research, I believed that I could not only heal my body from breast cancer treatment, but I could also help prevent a recurrence of my breast cancer. I was sold. I was willing to try anything that could increase the chances that I would be around to see my beautiful son, Cooper, grow up. I would become vegan, and even consume a diet of only raw vegan foods, if that was what it would take to get me healthy. I would start drinking a green juice every morning. I would eliminate all animal products from my diet, including my beloved cheese.

GETTING STARTED

I dove into the deep end, immediately ordering a simple two-speed Breville juice fountain. I will never forget making my first green juice in my kitchen. My husband, Kirk, thought I was crazy. It was so green, but the smell of the "real" fruits and vegetables coming from my juicer was intoxicating. At first, I put an entire apple in my green juice each morning, but as time went by, I noticed that I was losing the sweet tooth that I had been known for my entire life (I never skipped dessert). The apple started tasting too sweet, so I gradually used less and less until I left it out altogether, drinking a simple combination of kale, cucumber, and celery. I would juice 32 ounces (946 ml) of these ingredients and head out the door each morning with what my friends came to call my "pond water."

The results of drinking a simple green juice every day were amazing. I had an incredible amount of energy all the time. My immune system—which had been completely wiped out by the chemotherapy— rebounded. My skin glowed, and my hair (which was finally growing back) was black and shiny once again. Mentally, I was sharp and clear. And

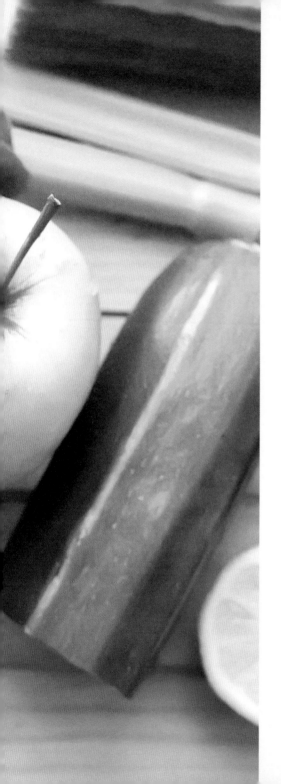

I was happy. For me, the daily flush of nutrients from my green juice was like the fountain of youth.

Over time, I realized that I no longer needed coffee and dropped it in favor of green tea. I also realized that I did not need anything else to eat until lunch. This created a mini juice fast each day, from dinner the night before until I ate solid food at lunch the next day. I found that this daily mini-fast helped my body to cleanse itself of toxins from bad eating. Nine years later, I still drink a green juice every day. I am convinced that it has changed the outcome of my life. I am not just surviving my breast cancer, but thriving in every way. I have more energy and drive than many of my friends and counterparts my age. I also require far less exercise to maintain my weight than my friends of a similar age. While I absolutely love and enjoy exercise, I work out regularly to feel good mentally and physically, not to maintain my weight. My weight is maintained by the smart food choices I am making. Since my body fully absorbs the nutrients consumed, I do not constantly feel hungry, and as a result, I naturally only consume the calories needed to maintain a normal weight.

My eyesight is also still remarkable. Despite the fact that I am at the age when most start using readers, I can still see perfectly without glasses.

Perhaps the most important thing I know with every fiber in my body is that I will not only be around to see my son Cooper grow up, but also to grow old with my husband. Unfortunately, breast cancer is one of those dreaded diseases from which you are never considered cured. It can rear its ugly head at any time, and often does for those of us diagnosed at such young ages. For that reason, I always stay the course. Each day when I drink my daily green juice, I reaffirm my dedication to my diet, to my healthy way of life, and to staying alive for Cooper and Kirk. They need me. Plain and simple. I am so blessed to be able to share my story and the healing power of green juice with the world. I am confident that this is the answer to the "why."

PAYING IT FORWARD

After years of spreading the gospel about drinking a daily green juice to my friends and family, in 2012, I decided that it was time to get serious about "paying it forward." Many of my friends and family members had already purchased juicers and started making a green juice every morning. While they all agreed that the health benefits they experienced were undeniable, after a few months they would ultimately put the juicer away, declaring that it was "too hard," "too messy," and "took too much time."

I soon realized that if I was going to keep my friends and family drinking a daily green juice, I was going to have to make it for them. So on December 1, 2012, I made sixty bottles of cold-pressed green juice and took it to the local farmers market in Austin, Texas. It sold out in less than two hours. So the next weekend, I made sixty more bottles and did it again. At the time, I was still working my day job as a corporate attorney, so I had to rope in my then-eight-year-old son and husband to help hand-label the bottles and support me at the farmers market. After selling out at two consecutive farmers markets, I realized that there was a serious need for ready-to-drink green juice made the way I make it (with mostly greens, low in fruit, and with no water added). In 2012, fresh green juice was only available in cities that were lucky enough to have a juice bar—or in New York and along the West Coast, where a small number of cold-pressed juice companies had launched locally.

I made it my mission to get a green juice into the hands of every American every day. And so it was that my company, Daily Greens, was born. After four short months, I left my corporate attorney job behind and dove headfirst into the business of making green juice available to anyone and everyone who would listen to me. Only five months after taking that very first batch to the farmers market, Daily Greens launched at Whole Foods Markets—and the rest is history. Today, Daily Greens juices are available coast to coast in thousands of retail outlets. See the website to find the location closest to you: www.drinkdailygreens.com/location.

During my own battle with breast cancer, I cofounded an organization in Texas known as the Pink Ribbon Cowgirls. It is a program that provides a social network and support services to young women battling breast cancer. The concept grew out of the support and companionship my sister and I were able to provide to each other during our two years of treatment together. Over the years, the Pink Ribbon Cowgirls have provided support and sisterhood to hundreds of young women battling breast cancer. Resources for such women are still scarce in this country—despite the increase of breast cancer in young women. For this reason, we set

aside a portion of the revenues at Daily Greens to help fund organizations that provide services to young women fighting breast cancer. In order to further this vision and mission, we will also be donating 1 percent of the royalties from this book to those organizations. If you have been touched by someone courageously battling breast cancer, I encourage you to visit our website and see how you can make a difference too: www.drinkdailygreens. com/we-give-back/.

I no longer ask myself, "Why me?" I know now that it was my destiny to battle breast cancer at thirty-three. It made me who I am today. It created in me a burning desire not only to help other young women facing this disease, but to help you, the reader of my book, to get healthy and stay healthy so you can thrive for the important people in your life.

WHY JUICE?

It was common for our ancient ancestors to eat up to six pounds (2.7 kg) of leaves per day. But in modern-day throwback "hunter-gatherer" diets, much emphasis is placed on the "hunting" of meat by our ancestors, and we forget that wild game kills were few and far between. While our ancestors mostly subsisted on leaves, berries, and nuts, today the standard American diet consists mostly of animal protein. According to the Produce for Better Health Foundation, nine out of ten Americans don't eat the recommended daily amount of fruits and vegetables. But these foods provide vital nutrients needed to fight disease and maintain good health. What's more, the majority of the standard American diet consists of cooked food, and cooking results in the loss of many of the nutrients in the scarce fruits and vegetables that we do consume. And with our modern, fast-paced lifestyle, who has time to eat six pounds of "leaves" a day?

So what is the solution? Juice! Juicing dark leafy greens, along with other vegetables and some fruit, into a green juice can provide in a single drink many of the nutrients that so many of us are not usually getting. The other benefit of juicing? You are condensing these nutrients into a liquid form that is immediately absorbed by the body, with very few of the nutrients lost through the digestive process.

THE TRUTH ABOUT VITAMIN SUPPLEMENTS

Did you know that our bodies absorb over 97 percent of the nutrients contained in raw vegetables and fruit? Compare that to vitamin supplements made in a laboratory, which have an absorption rate of 5 to 25 percent.

WHY GREEN JUICE?

Dark leafy greens offer higher concentrations of nutrients than many other vegetables and fruits. They are a rich source of minerals, including iron, calcium, potassium, and magnesium, as well as vitamins, including vitamins K, C, E, and many of the B vitamins. They also provide a variety of phytonutrients, including beta-carotene, lutein, and zeaxanthin, which help protect our cells from damage. Dark leafy greens even contain small amounts of omega-3 fats, which are good for you, playing a role in lowering triglyceride levels.

Perhaps the star of these nutrients is vitamin K. Two cups (40 g) of dark leafy greens provide more than the minimum daily recommended amount of vitamin K. Research cited by the American Cancer Society has provided evidence that this vitamin may be even more important than once thought—and many people do not get nearly enough of it. Not only is vitamin K essential for normal blood clotting, recent studies suggest that deficient levels of vitamin K are linked to an increased risk of some cancers. In addition, studies have revealed that vitamin K may have a role in keeping bones strong, especially in older people.

You might be wondering: *If dark leafy greens are so great, why not just juice kale?* Well, put simply, because it tastes like crap. However, by combining dark leafy greens with other green vegetables and some fruit and herbs, you can create a green juice that both tastes delicious and is full of nutrients that your body needs for long-term health.

One of the most frequent questions I am asked is: If you don't eat meat, how do you get calcium and iron? The answer is simple: I eat plants. Specifically, I consume dark leafy greens every day in the form of green juice and vegetable salads. Dark leafy greens such as spinach, kale, collard greens, watercress, and dandelion greens contain more iron than an equivalent serving of cow's milk while also providing a good amount of calcium.

My doctors require frequent bone-density tests and are always very surprised to note that my bone density is fantastic, given my plant-based diet and refusal to take nutrient and mineral supplements. They always tell me that whatever I am doing with my diet is certainly working and to keep up the good work.

WHY EAT SEASONALLY?

The different recipes featured in the different seasonal cleanses are based on my own philosophy for consuming fruits and vegetables that are in season or available from my local farmers market. There are three very important reasons to eat seasonally:

1. Ideally, fruits and vegetables are harvested when they are ripe. This is when they contain the highest level of nutrients they will ever contain during their life cycle.

2. Eating foods in season often means that you can select your produce from your local farmer or farmers market and lessen the environmental impact of shipping produce across the country.

3. Finally, eating seasonally will save you money. The price of produce is lower when it is in season and available locally.

ORGANIC PRODUCE

I recommend that your fruits and vegetables be organic to the greatest extent possible. I know they can cost a lot more at the grocery store, but I believe the benefits far outweigh the cost.

1. I find that organic produce tastes better.

2. While there is differing research on the topic, I believe that organic produce contains higher levels of nutrients (the Organic Trade Association at ota.com lists the results of several major scientific studies).

3. Produce that comes from organic farms does not contain pesticides and other poisons commonly used to kill insects and maximize production. As reported by the National Cancer Institute, it is many of these same pesticides that are now being linked to cancer, and which I personally hold responsible for my untimely battle with breast cancer.

4. Another important reason to buy organic is to support organic farmers, as they use sustainable farming practices that protect and rehabilitate the soil, as well as prevent further contamination of our environment by employing natural fertilizers and pest repellents instead of poisonous chemicals that contribute to the contamination of our groundwater, lakes, rivers, and oceans.

DR. WEIL'S "DIRTY DOZEN PLUS"

- Strawberries
- Spinach
- Kale
- Nectarines
- Apples
- Grapes
- Peaches
- Cherries
- Pears
- Tomatoes
- Celery
- Potatoes

Plus these two that may contain "highly toxic" insecticides:
- Hot peppers
- Blueberries (domestic)

If you are on a budget, I would highly recommend that—at a minimum—you consider purchasing organic versions of the produce that appears on the "dirty dozen" list. This is a list of the fruits and vegetables that retain the most residual poisons from pesticides used by non-organic farmers. Opposite is the 2019 list published by Dr. Andrew Weil, a health expert who is internationally recognized for his views on leading a healthy lifestyle, his philosophy of healthy aging, and his critique of the future of medicine and health care.

EQUIPMENT NEEDED FOR JUICING

Here is a list of equipment you should make sure you have at home to start juicing.

HOME JUICER

While I own several high-end expensive juicers, I almost always use my simple Breville Juice Fountain to make green juice at home. It is inexpensive in the juicing world, works wonderfully, and is easy to use. I recommend the two-speed version, which will allow you to alter the speed depending on the produce you are juicing. Using the recommended speed will prevent waste. The fountain opening allows you to put larger pieces of fruit and vegetables into the juicer, thus requiring less time for cutting your produce into small portions. It also breaks down into three parts for easy washing. As of late, there are a number of juicers on the market that attempt to bridge the gap between cold-pressed juicers, like the professional-grade Norwalk, and the centrifugal juicers like the Breville. I have experimented with several of these, including the Huron. While they are nice and may extract slightly more nutrients, they do slow down the process of making juice. I encourage you to do some research on the best juicer for your budget.

A word of caution: Do not attempt to use a blender as a juicer. It just cannot be done. A blender retains all the fiber and, thus, works for making a green smoothie, but not a green juice.

HIGH-SPEED BLENDER

You will need a blender to make the green smoothie and raw soup recipes in this book. I am very passionate about my Vitamix. I could not live without it. When trying to break down raw produce into a creamy texture for smoothies, I find it is the only blender that truly gets the job done. I know it comes with a high price tag, so feel free to substitute a regular high-speed blender.

COLANDER
Juicing involves washing large quantities of fruits and vegetables, both for your juices and for the vegetarian recipes. A large colander will make this process easier.

SHARP KNIVES
You will also be chopping up large quantities of fruits and vegetables, so a set of sharp knives is highly recommended. If your knives are dull, you can sharpen them yourself or take them to a store that does knife sharpening before you begin your cleanse. Take extra care when using ultra-sharp knives—you don't want to hurt yourself!

SALAD SPINNER (OPTIONAL)
There are number of recipes for large salads, and a salad spinner can make it easier to prepare your greens. If you don't already have one, a colander to drain your washed lettuce will work just fine as a substitute.

SPIRALIZER AND MANDOLIN (OPTIONAL)
These tools can come in handy for preparing paper-thin veggie slices (on the mandolin) or spaghetti-thin vegetable curls (on the spiralizer). Both are inexpensive and can easily be found online or in retail stores carrying kitchenware.

SIMPLE GREEN JUICE FORMULA

My hope for you is that once you try juicing, you will crave a morning green juice as much as I do. In case you want to experiment with your own recipes, here are some guidelines for the perfect proportions for making a fantastic green juice.

2 PARTS SWEET JUICY GREENS
(CELERY, CUCUMBER, ROMAINE [COS])

1 PART FRUIT
(APPLE, WATERMELON, PEAR, PINEAPPLE)

⅔ PART DARK LEAFY GREENS
(KALE, SPINACH, COLLARD GREENS)

⅓ PART HERB
(MINT, BASIL, CILANTRO, PARSLEY)

New Year ❋

Is there a better time of year to begin juicing? If you're anything like the majority of the world, you've indulged and enjoyed the wonderful foods of the holidays, and you're ready for a reset. Here's a convenient shopping list for making all eleven of the energizing superfood juices in this section.

JUICE SHOPPING LIST

VEGETABLES	QUANTITY
CARROT	1 large
CELERY	3 heads
CUCUMBERS	4 medium
GINGER ROOT	½-inch (13mm) piece
GREEN CABBAGE	1 small head
KALE	1 bunch
ROMAINE	1 head
SPINACH	3 bunches or 1 large box, pre-washed
SWISS CHARD	1 bunch
WATERCRESS	1 bunch

FRUIT	QUANTITY
BANANA	1 large
GRANNY SMITH APPLE	1 medium
GRAPEFRUIT	1 medium
GREEN GRAPES	1 bunch
KIWI	1 small
LEMON	1 medium
LIME	1 small
MANGO	1 small
PINEAPPLE	½ whole
ORANGES	2 medium

HERBS	QUANTITY
BASIL	1 bunch
CILANTRO (CORIANDER)	1 bunch
MINT	1 bunch
PARSLEY	1 bunch

OTHER	QUANTITY
BLUE-GREEN ALGAE (E3-Live AFA)	1 small container of powdered supplement
CAYENNE PEPPER	small amount
SALT (HIMALAYAN PINK)	1 shaker of whole crystals
VANILLA EXTRACT	1 small vile

NEW YEAR MORNING GREEN JUICE

My favorite part of the morning is preparing my morning green juice. This morning juice is an essential part of my day. And it can be an essential part of yours too!

INGREDIENTS

* ❄ 4 or 5 romaine (cos) leaves
* ❄ 2 or 3 kale leaves
* ❄ ¼ pineapple or 1½ cups (250 g) pineapple chunks (fresh or frozen)
* ❄ Handful cilantro (coriander) leaves (from 3 or 4 stems)

METHOD

1. Wash the romaine (cos), kale, and cilantro.
2. Top and tail the pineapple, peel it, and cut into pieces that will fit through your juicer.
3. Run all ingredients through your juicer, scrape off foam (if desired), and enjoy!

SHAUNA'S GREEN SMOOTHIE

In my hometown of Austin, Texas, I am well known for this green smoothie. I started making it over nine years ago at the beginning of my own journey back to good health. I used to take a pitcher of it to my workout to share with everyone in my fitness class. They thought I was crazy for asking them to drink a smoothie that was a brilliant shade of green. Plus, my gym already had a smoothie bar—but they made the type of smoothies popular at the time, with berries or bananas, some form of milk (usually cow's milk), and a big scoop of animal-based protein powder. Since they did not make anything that I would drink, I brought my own to share. Once folks got past the "greenness" of this smoothie, it was a universal crowd-pleaser.

INGREDIENTS

- ❋ Big handful spinach (⅔ bunch)
- ❋ Handful mint leaves (from 3 to 4 stems)
- ❋ ¼-inch (6 mm) piece ginger root
- ❋ ½ banana (fresh or frozen)
- ❋ ½ cup (88 g) mango chunks or sliced peaches (fresh or frozen)
- ❋ ½ cup (120 ml) filtered water

METHOD

1. Wash the spinach, mint, and ginger root.
2. Add all ingredients to your high-speed blender or Vitamix, and blend on High until smooth and creamy.
3. Add more water, if needed, to obtain desired consistency for drinking.

BANANA ORANGE SMOOTHIE

It does not get any more basic than combining spinach, banana, and orange into a super-simple green smoothie. I love making this one in the winter, when oranges are in season and a bit sweeter. It takes less than five minutes to prepare, so this is a great go-to recipe when you are in a hurry in the morning.

INGREDIENTS

* ❄ Big handful of spinach (⅔ bunch)
* ❄ ½ banana (fresh or frozen)
* ❄ 1 medium orange or two small oranges
* ❄ 1 cup (235 ml) filtered water
* ❄ ½ cup (88g) mango chunks or sliced peaches (fresh or frozen)
* ❄ ½ cup (120ml) filtered water

METHOD

1. Wash the spinach.
2. Add all ingredients to your high-speed blender or Vitamix, and blend on High until smooth and creamy.
3. Add more water, if needed, to obtain desired consistency for drinking.

ORANGE CILANTRO JUICE

Combining an orange with your greens offers a healthy boost to traditional orange juice. It adds loads of Vitamin C to your green juice, which is already packed with vitamin A and all the B vitamins, making this recipe a nutritious (and delicious!) powerhouse.

INGREDIENTS

- ❋ 4 or 5 kale leaves
- ❋ 2 or 3 romaine (cos) leaves
- ❋ Handful cilantro (coriander) leaves (from 3 or 4 stems; optional)
- ❋ 1 orange

METHOD

1. Wash the kale, romaine, and cilantro.
2. Peel the orange and cut into pieces that will fit in your juicer.
3. Run all ingredients through your juicer, scrape off foam (if desired), and enjoy.

APPLE KIWI GINGER JUICE

Kiwi is a fun and unusual choice that gives your green juice a tropical twist. I love incorporating tropical fruits into my juices in the winter to help chase away the winter blues. It makes me feel like I have taken a momentary beach vacation on a faraway island.

INGREDIENTS

- ❋ ½ Granny Smith apple
- ❋ 2 or 3 romaine (cos) leaves
- ❋ Handful watercress (⅓ bunch)
- ❋ ¼-inch (6 mm) piece ginger root
- ❋ 1 kiwi

METHOD

1. Wash the apple, romaine leaves, watercress, and ginger.
2. Peel the kiwi and cut into pieces that will fit through the juicer.
3. Cut and core the apple and cut into pieces that will fit through your juicer.
4. Run all ingredients through your juicer, scrape off foam (if desired), and enjoy

VANILLA GRAPEFRUIT JUICE

INGREDIENTS

* ❄ 1 cucumber
* ❄ 3 or 4 kale leaves
* ❄ Handful cilantro (coriander) leaves (from 3 or 4 stems)
* ❄ ½ grapefruit
* ❄ ¼ lime
* ❄ 1 tablespoon pure vanilla extract

METHOD

1. Wash the cucumber, kale, and cilantro.
2. Peel the grapefruit and lime and cut each into quarters that will fit through your juicer.
3. Run all ingredients through your juicer and scrape off foam (if desired).
4. Stir in the vanilla, and enjoy this wonderful combination!

I adore this juice. It uses many of my favorite flavors in an unexpected combination that is truly delicious. The vanilla with grapefruit adds a nice touch of sweetness without adding calories.

GRAPE WATERCRESS JUICE

Watercress is another of my favorite green superfoods. Watercress grows naturally in springs and along the riverbanks of slow-moving rivers. I grew up on a farm with many large springs that came bubbling up from the ground and served as our source of drinking water. Watercress grew prolifically at the source of all the springs, and as a young girl I used to harvest watercress straight out of the spring, and my mother would toss it into our salads for an interesting spicy flavor.

INGREDIENTS

* ❋ 1 cup (150 g) green grapes
* ❋ Big handful spinach (⅔ bunch)
* ❋ 1 cucumber
* ❋ Handful watercress (⅓ bunch)
* ❋ Handful basil (3 or 4 leaves)

METHOD

1. Wash the grapes, spinach, cucumber, watercress, and basil.
2. Run all ingredients through your juicer, scrape off foam (if desired), and enjoy!

SUPERFOOD HIGHLIGHT

WATERCRESS

Watercress is a great source of antioxidants, vitamin C, beta-carotene, folate, potassium, and phosphorous, and contains more calcium than milk and more iron than spinach. It is cultivated by organic farmers and available in most grocery stores on a year-round basis.

Preparing watercress is simple: After trimming the stems, rinse the greens in cold water and dry on a paper towel or in a salad spinner. Use immediately, or store in

a closed container in the refrigerator for up to 4 days. Watercress can take the place of lettuce in any salad, sandwich, or other recipe, and can be used as a nutritious garnish. It also makes a wonderful ingredient in a green juice.

CARROT CHARD JUICE

Swiss chard has been ranked by the World's Healthiest Foods Organization as the second-most nutrient-rich vegetable in the world (after spinach). Most Swiss chard has a bit of red coloring, so it may stain your juicer or, if too strong, even turn your juice a faint brown. Don't be alarmed! To the contrary, know that you are getting a wonderful dose of one of the most nutrient-dense foods on the planet.

INGREDIENTS

- ❄ 1 large carrot or 2 small carrots, top and bottom removed
- ❄ 4 or 5 celery ribs, bottoms removed
- ❄ 3 or 4 Swiss chard leaves
- ❄ ¼ lemon, peeled

METHOD

① Wash the carrot, celery, and chard leaves.
② Run all ingredients through your juicer, scrape off foam (if desired), and enjoy!

SUPERFOOD HIGHLIGHT

SWISS CHARD

Swiss chard is one of those wonderful super greens full of antioxidants, including kaempferol, the same phytonutrient found in broccoli and kale. Swiss chard is also a cousin to the beet family, and it contains phytonutrients found in beets called betalains, which have been shown to provide antioxidant, anti-inflammatory, and detoxification support. Baby Swiss chard is also a great addition to salads, as it mixes well with other super greens like baby spinach and watercress.

To prepare Swiss chard, just rinse before running it through your juicer, stems and all.

SPICY WINTER JUICE

In the midst of the cold of winter, a little spice can be a big pick-me-up. I've found that the winter blues are no match for a hot kick of cayenne in my juice—it wakes up my taste buds and offers a jolt to my body and mind.

INGREDIENTS

* ❄ 3 or 4 celery ribs, bottoms removed
* ❄ Big handful spinach (⅔ bunch)
* ❄ ⅛ pineapple or 1 cup (165 g) pineapple chunks (fresh or frozen)
* ❄ ⅛ teaspoon Himalayan pink salt
* ❄ Pinch cayenne pepper (⅛ teaspoon or less)

METHOD

1. Wash the celery and spinach.
2. Top and tail the pineapple, peel it, and cut into pieces that will fit through your juicer.
3. Run the vegetables and pineapple through your juicer and scrape off foam (if desired).
4. Season with salt and cayenne, and enjoy!

CABBAGE PARSLEY JUICE

Cabbage is related to the broccoli family, and in addition to containing high quantities of vitamin C and other antioxidants, it contains a variety of nutrients that promote overall stomach and intestinal health.

INGREDIENTS

- ❋ 2 or 3 green cabbage leaves
- ❋ 3 to 5 celery ribs, bottoms removed
- ❋ 1 cucumber
- ❋ Handful parsley leaves (from 3 or 4 stems)
- ❋ ¼ lemon, peeled (optional)

METHOD

1. Wash the cabbage, celery, cucumber, and parsley.
2. If you need to cut the greenness, use ¼ lemon. If not, skip it.
3. Run all ingredients through your juicer, scrape off foam (if desired), and enjoy!

BLUE-GREEN ALGAE JUICE
(AKA HAPPY JUICE)

Freshwater blue-green algae (Aphanizomanon flos-aquae, or AFA) is an ancient, nutrient-packed plant sold in powder form at natural food stores. When I add it to my juice, it increases my energy and boosts my mood, so I call it "happy juice."

INGREDIENTS

* ❈ 1 cucumber
* ❈ 3 to 5 celery ribs, bottoms removed
* ❈ 3 or 4 kale leaves
* ❈ ½ lemon, peeled (optional)
* ❈ 1 to 2 teaspoons blue-green algae (I like E3Live brand)

METHOD

1. Wash the cucumber, celery, and kale.
2. If you need to cut the greenness, use ½ lemon. If not, skip it.
3. Run all vegetables and lemon through your juicer and scrape off foam (if desired).
4. Add the algae, and enjoy!

SUPERFOOD HIGHLIGHT

FRESHWATER BLUE-GREEN ALGAE

Composed of almost 70 percent protein, blue-green algae also offers dozens upon dozens of vitamins and minerals as well as essential fatty acids. In particular, it's loaded with all the crucial B vitamins, which help improve brain function, stabilize moods, and generate red blood cells for improved vitality—among their many other wonderful benefits. E-3Live is a wonderful source, harvesting and drying the algae naturally to preserve its nutrients.

VEGGIE HAND ROLLS

These are such a fun addition to sushi night. Plus, they're very filling. I discovered this recipe after struggling to make vegetable sushi rolls that were not all damp and droopy—a tall order when you eliminate cooked rice from the mix. I substituted a romaine leaf for the rice and found that it adds a wonderful crispy texture to a sushi roll.

INGREDIENTS

- ✳ 3 nori seaweed sheets
- ✳ 6 small heart of romaine (cos) leaves
- ✳ 1 to 2 tablespoons raw miso paste
- ✳ 1 avocado, thinly sliced
- ✳ 1 medium carrot, thinly sliced or shredded
- ✳ ½ cucumber, peeled and thinly sliced
- ✳ 1 cup (50 g) sprouts (any kind)
- ✳ Sea salt, to taste
- ✳ 1-inch (2.5 cm) piece ginger root
- ✳ 1 to 2 tablespoons raw soy sauce (nama shoyu), for dipping

METHOD

1. Cut the nori sheets in half with kitchen scissors and place on a cutting board with the shiny sides down.

2. Place a romaine leaf on each nori sheet, with the tip of the leaf aligned with the corner of the nori.

3. Coat the inside of each leaf with miso paste.

4. Evenly distribute avocado, carrot, and cucumber onto each nori sheet.

5. Add a few sprouts on top and season with salt.

6. Wet the edge of one nori sheet and roll up tightly. Repeat with remaining sheets.

7. Peel the fresh ginger root and slice thinly, then arrange on plate as a garnish. Serve with soy sauce for dipping.

RAW ZUCCHINI SPAGHETTI

Making spaghetti out of raw zucchini is super easy with a spiralizer, a very inexpensive tool that makes raw cooking a lot more fun. I highly recommend purchasing one, and then try this fun recipe that will really satiate you.

INGREDIENTS

- ✳ 5 or 6 ripe tomatoes, cut into chunks
- ✳ ¼ sweet onion, cut into chunks
- ✳ 2 garlic cloves, peeled
- ✳ Handful fresh basil (6 or 7 leaves)
- ✳ 1 or 2 stems fresh oregano
- ✳ 1 to 2 tablespoons extra-virgin olive oil
- ✳ Sea salt, to taste
- ✳ Freshly ground black pepper, to taste
- ✳ 1 or 2 small zucchinis

METHOD

1. To create a fantastic raw marinara, in a high-speed blender or Vitamix, combine tomatoes, onion, garlic gloves, basil, oregano, and olive oil. Pulse until smooth, then add salt and black pepper.

2. If you have one, use a spiralizer to create spaghetti-like curls out of the zucchinis. If you don't have one, just shred the zucchini with a carrot peeler, peeling and all, or finely chop into small sticks.

3. Arrange the zucchini "spaghetti" in a bowl and top with the marinara sauce.

RAW CAULIFLOWER SOUP

Time for some tasty raw soup. I highly recommend using a Vitamix; however, a high-speed blender will work as well. I definitely recommend the extra step of heating this up a bit on the stove to warm up your tummy. Food is still considered raw as long as it is not heated above 115°F (50°C). Above this temperature, the vegetables start losing nutrients to the heat.

INGREDIENTS

- ¼ cup (35 g) pine nuts
- 1 cup (235 ml) water
- ½ head of cauliflower, cut into florets
- 1 garlic clove
- ¼ sweet onion
- 1 to 2 teaspoons Italian seasoning
- 2 to 3 teaspoons extra-virgin olive oil
- Sea salt, to taste
- Freshly ground black pepper, to taste
- Parsley leaves, to garnish

METHOD

1. Place the pine nuts and water in the Vitamix or high-speed blender, and run on High for a minute or two to create a creamy base.

2. Add the cauliflower florets, garlic, and onion. Blend until the texture is smooth.

3. Add the Italian seasoning and olive oil, and season with the salt and pepper. Blend on High until smooth, adding more water as needed until it reaches desired consistency.

4. If you would like a warm soup while keeping it raw, pour it into a saucepan on the stove and heat over the lowest possible temperature. Stir constantly until the soup is warm to the touch, and remove immediately. Ladle into a bowl and garnish with parsley and black pepper.

SIMPLE WINTER SALAD

This salad is so simple and delicious. I often use it as a base for more complicated salads, as it contains such great building blocks. However, it's also great just as it is.

INGREDIENTS

* ❄ I head butter lettuce, torn or chopped
* ❄ I medium carrot, shredded
* ❄ ½ cucumber, peeled and thinly sliced
* ❄ 2 or 3 green onions, thinly sliced
* ❄ Handful watercress, stems removed (½ bunch; optional)
* ❄ I tablespoon whole-grain mustard
* ❄ I tablespoon raw apple cider vinegar
* ❄ 2 tablespoons extra-virgin olive oil
* ❄ Sea salt, to taste
* ❄ Freshly ground black pepper, to taste
* ❄ Pinch cayenne

METHOD

① Combine the butter lettuce, shredded carrot, cucumber slices, and green onions in a large bowl. Add watercress, if using, and toss well.

② To make the dressing, whisk together the mustard, apple cider vinegar, and olive oil in a separate small bowl. Season with salt and black pepper to taste, add cayenne, and whisk to combine.

③ Sprinkle salt onto the salad, pour dressing over the top, and toss gently.

PORTOBELLO MUSHROOM SANDWICH

I love grilled portobello mushrooms, and they make a very hearty sandwich with tons of flavor. This recipe has a few more steps than my usual recipes, but trust me, it's worth it!

INGREDIENTS

* 1 portobello mushroom
* 1 tablespoon balsamic vinegar
* 3 to 4 tablespoons extra-virgin olive oil, plus more for brushing and if needed for the pesto
* ½ red bell pepper (red capsicum), sliced
* Sea salt, to taste
* Freshly ground black pepper, to taste
* 1 big bunch basil
* ¼ cup (35 g) pine nuts
* 2 slices whole-grain bread (preferably sprouted grain)

METHOD

1. Preheat the oven to 400°F (200°C).
2. To marinate the mushroom, pour balsamic vinegar and 1 tablespoon of olive oil into the center of the upside-down mushroom and let stand for a few minutes.
3. Brush the bell pepper slices with olive oil and season with salt and black pepper.
4. Place the mushroom and red pepper into a baking dish, cover with foil, and bake for about 20 minutes, or until both are tender.
5. To make a vegan pesto, combine the basil, pine nuts, and remaining 2 to 3 tablespoons olive oil in a high-speed blender or Vitamix. Blend on high until smooth, approximately 1 minute. Season with salt and pepper. Add more oil as needed to reach desired consistency.
6. When ready to assemble your sandwich, toast the bread and coat each slice with pesto.
7. Layer the mushroom and roasted red peppers onto one slice of bread, close up your sandwich, and enjoy!

SWEET POTATO
ASPARAGUS CASSEROLE

When you are vegan, you learn that it is best to bring your own dish to all potluck events, especially brunch events in Texas, which tend to mostly consist of bacon and egg tacos. My good friend Jennifer Anderson introduced me to this wonderful plant-based casserole, which is always a huge hit at potlucks, particularly at brunch, but also makes for a very filling dinner dish. Allow yourself about forty-five minutes baking time, but it takes less than ten minutes to prep.

INGREDIENTS

- ❄ 2 sweet potatoes, peeled and cubed
- ❄ 1 bunch green asparagus, cut into 3-inch pieces
- ❄ 3 or 4 garlic cloves, minced
- ❄ Handful fresh thyme leaves (from 2 or 3 sprigs), finely chopped
- ❄ 1 or 2 plant-based sausages (such as Field Roast brand)
- ❄ 3 to 4 tablespoons extra-virgin olive oil
- ❄ Sea salt, to taste
- ❄ Freshly ground black pepper, to taste

METHOD

1. Preheat the oven to 425°F (220°C).
2. Arrange the sweet potatoes in a glass casserole dish.
3. Arrange the asparagus on top of the sweet potatoes, then sprinkle with garlic and thyme.
4. Break up the sausage into bite-size chunks and sprinkle over the top of the asparagus.
5. Drizzle olive oil over the casserole, distributing evenly across the surface. Season with salt and black pepper.
6. Place foil over the casserole and bake for 45 minutes, or until the sweet potatoes are soft. Remove foil and bake a few more minutes until everything is a bit crispy.

WARM SPINACH AND EGGS

Although I don't eat eggs myself anymore, I do prepare them frequently for my husband and son. Eggs are a wonderful source of protein. Out of all the animal proteins, they are the most easily digested and assimilated by the body. Plus, it's fun to eat eggs for dinner instead of for breakfast! Skip the toast and eat these delicious eggs with vegetables instead.

INGREDIENTS

- ❅ 2 or 3 eggs
- ❅ Dash cayenne pepper (optional)
- ❅ 2 tablespoons olive oil, divided
- ❅ 1 green onion, thinly sliced
- ❅ 1 or 2 garlic cloves, minced
- ❅ 1 bunch spinach, stems removed, or 1 bag baby spinach

METHOD

1. Whisk the eggs and add a dash of cayenne if you like spice.
2. Heat 1 tablespoon of olive oil in a large skillet over medium heat. Scramble the eggs, being sure not to overcook them. Set aside on a plate.
3. In the same pan, add the remaining tablespoon olive oil, green onions, and garlic, and cook for 1 minute, or until slightly brown.
4. Add the spinach and cook for a minute or two, until wilted but not fully cooked.
5. Arrange the spinach on the plate of scrambled eggs, and enjoy!

Spring

Spring is one of the best seasons to begin juicing. Why? Well, there's a reason they call it spring cleaning! After all, a winter spent indulging in comfort food and cozying up in warm sweaters would make anyone lethargic and desperate for an energy boost. Here's a convenient shopping list for making all ten of the energizing superfood smoothies and juices in this section.

JUICE SHOPPING LIST

VEGETABLES	QUANTITY
	1 stalk
BOK CHOY	4 medium
CARROTS	2 heads
CELERY	1 bunch
COLLARD GREENS	7 medium
CUCUMBERS	¼-inch (6mm) piece
GINGER ROOT	1 bunch
KALE	1 head
ROMAINE (COS)	4 bunches or 2 large boxes, pre-washed
SPINACH	

FRUIT	QUANTITY
AVOCADO	1 small
BANANA	1 meduim
FUJI APPLES	2 medium
KIWIS	2 medium
LEMON	1 medium
LIME	1 small
PEARS	3 medium
PINEAPPLE	½ whole
STRAWBERRIES	1 pint

HERBS	QUANTITY
BASIL	1 bunch
CILANTRO (CORIANDER)	1 bunch
MINT	1 bunch
PARSLEY	1 bunch

OTHER	QUANTITY
VANILLA EXTRACT (PURE)	1 small vile

SPRING MORNING GREEN JUICE

My favorite part of the morning: preparing my morning green juice. As you can probably tell by now, this morning juice is an essential part of my day. And it can be an essential part of yours too!

INGREDIENTS

- 1 cucumber
- Big handful spinach (⅔ bunch)
- 1 pear
- Handful basil (3 or 4 leaves)

METHOD

1. Wash the cucumber, spinach, pear, and basil.
2. Cut and core the pear and cut into pieces that will fit through your juicer.
3. Run all ingredients through your juicer, scrape off foam (if desired), and enjoy!

GLOWING SKIN SMOOTHIE

The ingredients in this smoothie all promote beautiful glowing skin, especially the kiwi. If you want to switch things up a bit, it's fun to swap regular water for coconut water. Doing this will add electrolytes to your smoothie while offering a fun tropical taste.

INGREDIENTS

- Big handful spinach (⅔ bunch)
- I small avocado or ½ large avocado
- ½ banana (fresh or frozen)
- 2 kiwi
- I cup (235 ml) filtered water (or coconut water)

METHOD

1. Wash the spinach.
2. Remove the flesh from the avocado.
3. Add all ingredients to your high-speed blender or Vitamix, and blend on High until smooth and creamy.
4. Add more water if needed to obtain desired consistency for drinking.

PINEAPPLE MINT JUICE

I always love the combination of pineapple and mint. Mint, in particular, really wakes up my taste buds; it's so aromatic and adds a refreshing kick to any green juice.

INGREDIENTS

- ◊ 1 cucumber
- ◊ Big handful spinach (⅔ bunch)
- ◊ ½ Fuji apple
- ◊ Handful mint (3 or 4 leaves)
- ◊ ⅛ pineapple or 1 cup (165 g) pineapple chunks (fresh or frozen)

METHOD

1. Wash the cucumber, spinach, apple, and mint.
2. Cut and core the apple and cut into pieces that will fit in your juicer.
3. Top and tail the pineapple, peel it, and cut into pieces that will fit through your juicer.
4. Run all ingredients through your juicer, scrape off foam (if desired), and enjoy!

CARROT CILANTRO JUICE

Carrots have so many wonderful nutrients, but like fruit, they contain a lot of natural sugar. Thanks to their natural sweetness, they are a great substitute for fruit in a green juice—but be careful not to add too many, as they will turn your green juice a dusky brown color. I love this recipe's combination of carrots and cilantro.

INGREDIENTS

- ◊ 4 or 5 small carrots, tops and bottoms removed
- ◊ 1 cucumber
- ◊ 4 or 5 kale leaves
- ◊ Handful cilantro (coriander) leaves (from 3 to 4 stems; optional, but recommended)
- ◊ ¼ lime, peeled

METHOD

1. Wash the carrots, cucumber, kale and cilantro.
2. Cut the long stems off the cilantro leaves.
3. Run all ingredients through your juicer, and scrape off foam (if desired).

PEAR APPLE GINGER JUICE

Fresh ginger root is wonderful in vegetable stir-fry dishes, and it adds a wonderful touch of spice to any juice or smoothie. You can find it year-round in the produce section of your local market.

INGREDIENTS

- ½ Fuji apple
- ½ pear
- 5 kale leaves
- 5 celery ribs, bottoms removed
- ¼-inch (6 mm) piece ginger root (optional)
- ¼ lemon, peeled (optional)

METHOD

1. Wash the apple, pear, kale, celery, and ginger.
2. Cut and core the apple and pear and cut into pieces that will fit through your juicer.
3. Run all ingredients through your juicer, scrape off foam (if desired), and enjoy!

SPRING

CARROT PINEAPPLE JUICE

Carrots make a great substitute for fruit in a juice, adding sweetness and loads of vitamin A, which promotes good eyesight. They also combine deliciously with pineapple for a perfect hint of sweetness.

INGREDIENTS

- ⬦ 1 cucumber
- ⬦ 2 carrots, tops and bottoms removed
- ⬦ 3 celery ribs, bottoms removed
- ⬦ 4 or 5 kale leaves
- ⬦ ⅛ pineapple or 1 cup (165 g) pineapple chunks (fresh or frozen)

METHOD

1. Wash the cucumber, carrots, celery, and kale.
2. Top and tail the pineapple, peel it, and cut into pieces that will fit through your juicer.
3. Run all ingredients through your juicer, scrape off foam (if desired), and enjoy!

BOK CHOY BASIL JUICE

Bok choy is another veggie that makes an early appearance at the spring farmers market. It is very satiating, especially when I'm craving Asian food.

INGREDIENTS

- 1 cucumber
- 1 head bok choy
- Big handful spinach (⅔ bunch)
- Handful basil (3 or 4 leaves)
- ½ lemon, peeled (optional)

METHOD

1. Wash the cucumber, bok choy, spinach, and basil.
2. If you need to cut the greenness, use ½ lemon. If not, skip it.
3. Run all ingredients through your juicer, scrape off foam (if desired), and enjoy!

VANILLA PEAR JUICE

I am always in search of a way to add sweetness to my green juice recipes without adding calories. One day, I decided to add some vanilla, and I fell in love. It adds a refreshing note of sweetness and combines so well with the pear and cilantro.

INGREDIENTS

- ❀ 1 pear
- ❀ 1 cucumber
- ❀ Big handful spinach
  (⅔ bunch)
- ❀ Handful cilantro (coriander)
  leaves (from 3 or 4
  stems; optional, but
  recommended)
- ❀ ¼ lime, peeled
- ❀ 2 teaspoons pure
  vanilla extract

METHOD

1. Wash the pear, cucumber, spinach, and cilantro.
2. Cut and core the pear and cut into pieces that will fit in your juicer.
3. Run all ingredients except vanilla through your juicer and scrape off foam (if desired).
4. Add the vanilla extract, stir, and enjoy!

SUPER GREEN JUICE

If you are looking for a sugar-free juice and are ready to go all green, this is the juice for you! This juice contains an amazing superfood—collard greens.

SUPERFOOD HIGHLIGHT

COLLARD GREENS

Collard greens can be substituted for other dark leafy greens in any green juice and offer some fantastic health benefits. Not only do collard greens help lower cholesterol, they also boast anti-inflammatory and detoxification powers. They're loaded with crucial antioxidants in the form of manganese and vitamins C, A, and E, as well as anti-inflammatory agents, vitamin K and omega-3 fatty acids.

INGREDIENTS

- 1 cucumber
- 3 celery ribs, bottoms removed
- 3 romaine (cos) leaves
- 2 collard green leaves
- Handful parsley leaves (from 3 or 4 stems)
- ½ lemon, peeled (optional)

METHOD

1. Wash the cucumber, celery, romaine, collard green leaves, and parsley.
2. If you need to cut the greenness, use ½ lemon. If not, skip it.
3. Run all ingredients through your juicer, scrape off foam (if desired), and enjoy!

STRAWBERRY PINEAPPLE MINT JUICE

Strawberries make a wonderful addition to a juice. They are chock-full of vitamin C and many other essential nutrients and antioxidants. For parents out there, my son loves strawberries and is fond of this green juice, so it's kid-tested!

INGREDIENTS

- 5 strawberries
- Big handful spinach (⅔ bunch)
- 4 romaine (cos) leaves
- ½ apple
- Handful mint (3 or 4 leaves)
- ⅛ pineapple or 1 cup (165 g) pineapple chunks (fresh or frozen)

METHOD

1. Wash the strawberries, spinach, romaine, apple, and mint.
2. Cut and core the apple and cut into pieces that will fit through your juicer.
3. Top and tail the pineapple, peel it, and cut into pieces that will fit through your juicer.
4. Run all ingredients through your juicer, scrape off foam (if desired) and enjoy!

SALSA AND VEGGIES

Salsa is easy to make in a high-speed blender or a Vitamix. Once you have the basics down, try adding interesting ingredients, like pineapple, or substituting tomatillos for the roma tomatoes.

INGREDIENTS

SALSA

- ½ white (sweet) onion, roughly chopped
- ¼ bunch cilantro (coriander), leaves only
- 1 to 2 garlic cloves
- ½ jalapeño, seeded and roughly chopped
- 4 roma tomatoes, quartered
- Juice of ½ lime
- Sea salt, to taste
- Freshly ground black pepper, to taste

VEGGIES FOR DIPPING

- ½ cup (60 g) carrot sticks
- ½ cup (50 g) celery sticks
- ½ cup (45 g) sliced red bell pepper (red capsicum)

METHOD

1. Combine the onion, cilantro, garlic, and jalapeño in a high-speed blender or Vitamix, and run on high until minced.
2. Add tomatoes and lime juice, and pulse until it reaches desired consistency.
3. Season with salt and black pepper.
4. Dip the carrots, celery, and red peppers in the salsa, and enjoy!

ASIAN STIR-FRY

I came up with this recipe one day on the fly, when I didn't have time to hit the grocery store and only had a random assortment of vegetables in my crisper drawer. It turned out so great that this is one of my frequent standbys when I'm in a hurry and the fridge isn't fully stocked. I simply use what I have on hand and mix and match the veggies for a wonderful Asian-inspired stir-fry that comes out perfectly every time. This recipe uses my favorite veggies, but almost any vegetable can serve as an acceptable substitute. So, use what you've got and clean out your crisper drawer before those leftover veggies go bad.

INGREDIENTS

- ½ container firm tofu
- 3 tablespoons sesame oil, divided
- 3 tablespoons raw almond butter, divided
- 4 to 5 tablespoons raw soy sauce (nama shoyu), divided
- 2 garlic cloves, minced
- 1 tablespoon minced fresh ginger root
- 2 or 3 green onions, thinly sliced
- 1 head bok choy (or cabbage or zucchini), roughly chopped
- 3 mushrooms (any kind), roughly chopped
- 1 cup (70 g) broccoli florets, chopped
- ½ medium carrot, thinly sliced or shredded
- Dash cayenne, to taste (optional)
- Handful cilantro (coriander) leaves (from 5 or 6 stems), torn into pieces

METHOD

1. Squeeze the excess liquid from the tofu and cut into bite-size chunks.
2. Heat 1 tablespoon of sesame oil in a wok or large nonstick skillet over high heat.
3. Add 1 tablespoon of almond butter, 1 tablespoon of soy sauce, and tofu to the wok and stir until tofu is crispy on the outside. Remove from the wok and set aside.
4. Add remaining 2 tablespoons sesame oil, remaining 2 tablespoons almond butter, garlic, ginger, and green onions. Stir until crispy.
5. Add bok choy, mushrooms, broccoli, and carrots, and stir constantly.
6. After a couple minutes, add remaining 3 to 4 tablespoons soy sauce. If desired, sprinkle with cayenne to add spice.
7. Stir until vegetables are crispy but not fully cooked. (You don't want to cook all the nutrients out of your vegetables.) When vegetables are almost done, toss the tofu back into wok and stir until warm.
8. Remove from heat and serve garnished with cilantro.

RED CABBAGE
AND WALNUT SALAD

This fun and hearty salad came about as I was preparing for a hamburger cookout. I needed something to complement all the burgers and pickles, and this salad was an instant hit.

INGREDIENTS

- ½ head red cabbage, thinly sliced
- 1 or 2 green onions, thinly sliced
- 3 tablespoons extra-virgin olive oil
- 2 tablespoons whole-grain mustard
- 2 tablespoons raw apple cider vinegar
- Sea salt, to taste
- Freshly ground black pepper, to taste
- 2 tablespoons halved raw walnuts
- Maple syrup, for drizzling

METHOD

1. Combine the cabbage and green onions in a large bowl.
2. To make the vinaigrette, whisk together the olive oil, mustard, and apple cider vinegar in a separate medium bowl, and season with salt and black pepper.
3. Pour the vinaigrette over the cabbage mixture and toss well.
4. Top with walnuts, drizzle with maple syrup, and serve!

ASIAN SPRING SOBA NOODLES

Soba noodles are my go-to noodle because they are made from buckwheat and are therefore gluten-free. Even if you are not gluten intolerant, they are a lot easier to digest and much lighter than traditional pasta. I love to combine them with any vegetables, but I am especially inspired to do so with fresh spring vegetables and herbs for a fun Asian-inspired noodle bowl.

INGREDIENTS

- 1 package soba noodles
- Sea salt, for boiling water
- 1 cucumber, peeled and thinly sliced or shredded
- 1 small carrot, thinly sliced or shredded
- 1 green onion, thinly sliced
- ½-inch (13 mm) piece ginger root, minced
- 2 tablespoons sesame oil
- 1 tablespoon rice wine vinegar
- 1 tablespoon maple syrup
- 2 tablespoons raw soy sauce (nama shoyu)
- 1 tablespoon black sesame seeds
- Sprinkle red pepper flakes, to taste (optional)
- Handful mung bean sprouts
- Handful fresh basil (6 or 7 leaves), chopped
- Handful fresh cilantro (coriander) leaves (from 5 or 6 stems), chopped
- Handful fresh mint (6 or 7 leaves), chopped

METHOD

1. Boil the soba noodles according to the package directions, adding a bit of sea salt to really bring out the flavors. Drain and place in a large bowl.
2. Add the cucumber, carrot, and green onion to the soba noodles and toss to combine.
3. To make an Asian vinaigrette, whisk together the ginger root, sesame oil, rice wine vinegar, maple syrup, soy sauce, sesame seeds, and red pepper flakes, if you want a little spice, in a separate medium bowl.
4. Pour the dressing over the noodles and vegetables, and toss until everything is coated.
5. Add the mung bean sprouts and herbs to the noodle bowl and serve warm or chilled.

KALE ORANGE SALAD

I love the combination of oranges and pomegranate seeds in the winter with sweet winter kale. This salad is so fun to make with winter–early spring kale from the farmers market.

INGREDIENTS

- 1 orange
- 2 tablespoons extra-virgin olive oil
- 1-inch (2.5 cm) piece ginger root, minced
- 1 teaspoon agave nectar
- 4 or 5 kale leaves, torn into bite-size pieces
- Sea salt, to taste
- Freshly ground black pepper, to taste
- ½ lemon
- 1 pomegranate, seeds only
- ¼ cup (30 g) almond slivers

METHOD

1. Peel the orange and remove slices from membrane, collecting the juice as you do so. Set aside the orange slices.
2. To make the dressing, whisk together the orange juice, olive oil, ginger, and agave nectar in a small bowl. Set aside.
3. Place the kale leaves in a large bowl and season with salt and black pepper.
4. Squeeze lemon juice onto the kale leaves and massage the juice into the kale to break it down a bit.
5. Toss in orange slices, pomegranate seeds, and almond slivers.
6. Pour the dressing over the salad and toss gently. Season with more salt and black pepper, and enjoy!

SWEET COLLARD GREENS SALAD

This is such a fun salad. I was inspired to use collard greens in a salad when I ended up with a big bunch of unused collard greens from the farmers market. This turned out so fresh with a hint of sweetness. While I try to generally stay away from using vegan substitutes for animal products, I do love the products made by Follow Your Heart—in particular, their Vegenaise, which is a staple in my fridge.

INGREDIENTS

- 4 or 5 collard green leaves, thinly sliced
- ¼ cup (22 g) dried apple slices
- 2 tablespoons dried cranberries
- 2 tablespoons almond slivers
- 2 tablespoons vegan mayo (such as Vegenaise by Follow Your Heart brand)
- 2 tablespoons filtered water
- 1 tablespoon agave nectar, plus more if needed

METHOD

1. Toss together the collard greens, dried apples, dried cranberries, and almond slivers in a large bowl.

2. To make the dressing, combine the vegan mayo, water (to thin it out), and agave nectar (to sweeten it up). Whisk together and test it for sweetness. If more sweetness is desired, add a touch more agave nectar.

3. Pour the dressing over the salad and toss, making sure the collard leaves are coated well.

Summer ✽

Summer is a great season for juicing. If you've got an upcoming vacation or wedding that you'd like to look your best for, juicing is a great way to get all those fruits and veggies. Here's a convenient shopping list for making all eleven of the energizing superfood smoothies and juices in this section.

JUICE SHOPPING LIST

HERBS	QUANTITY
BASIL	1 bunch
CILANTRO (CORIANDER)	1 bunch
MINT	1 bunch

VEGETABLES	QUANTITY
CELERY	2 heads
COLLARD GREENS	1 bunch
CUCUMBERS	6 medium
DANDELION GREENS	1 bunch
GINGER ROOT	¼-inch (6mm) piece
KALE	1 bunch
SPINACH	5 bunches or 2 large boxes, pre-washed
WATERCRESS	1 bunch
YELLOW PEPPER (YELLOW CAPSICUM)	1 medium
ZUCCHINI	3 medium

FRUIT	QUANTITY
CANTALOUPE	1 small melon
HONEYDEW	1 snall melon
GREEN GRAPES	1 bunch
LEMON	1 medium
PEACHES	2 medium
PEAR	1 medium
PINEAPPLE	1 pint fresh pineapple chunks
WATERMELON	1 small melon

OTHER	QUANTITY
CHIA SEEDS	½ cup (80g)
SALT (HIMALAYAN PINK)	1 shaker of whole crystals

SUMMER MORNING GREEN JUICE

My favorite part of the morning: preparing my morning green juice. As you can probably tell by now, this morning juice is an essential part of my day. And it can be an essential part of yours too!

INGREDIENTS

❊ 1 cucumber

❊ 1 or 2 collard green leaves

❊ Handful fresh mint
  (3 or 4 leaves)

❊ 1½ cups (230 g)
  watermelon chunks

METHOD

① Wash the cucumber, collard green leaves, and mint.

② Run all ingredients through your juicer, scrape off foam (if desired), and enjoy!

STRAWBERRY PEACH SMOOTHIE

This smoothie is great for summer, combining two of my favorite summer fruits: strawberries and peaches. My son loves this one because it also combines two of his favorite fruits. I used to cut up both strawberries and peaches for him to eat raw, and then it hit me that I should be combining his two favorite flavors into a green smoothie.

INGREDIENTS

* Big handful spinach (⅔ bunch)
* ½ cup (100 g) sliced peaches (fresh or frozen)
* ½ cup (55 g) whole strawberries (fresh or frozen), stems removed
* 1 cup (235 ml) filtered water (or coconut water if desired)
* 1 to 2 tablespooons ground chia seeds (optional)

METHOD

1. Wash the spinach, peaches, and strawberries (if fresh).
2. Add all ingredients to your high-speed blender or Vitamix, and blend on High until smooth and creamy.
3. Add more water if needed to obtain desired consistency for drinking.

HONEYDEW GRAPE
SMOOTHIE

Green grapes and honeydew melon combine so well to form a super-sweet base for a smoothie. If you are looking for a boost of protein and electrolytes, add a couple spoonfuls of ground chia seeds.

INGREDIENTS

- ❀ 3 or 4 kale leaves
- ❀ ½ cup (75 g) green grapes
- ❀ ½ cup (90 g) honeydew melon chunks
- ❀ ½ cup (120 ml) filtered water
- ❀ 2 tablespoons ground chia seeds (optional)

METHOD

1. Wash the kale and grapes.
2. Add all ingredients to your high-speed blender or Vitamix, and blend on High until smooth and creamy.
3. Add more water if needed to obtain desired consistency for drinking.

MELON MINT JUICE

Several years ago, my sister turned me onto the benefit of consuming chia seeds for hydration. She would put them in a Mason jar with water, a little lime, and Stevia to soak overnight. She would drink it the next morning after her run, to rehydrate and replenish. I tried it a few times and liked it so much that I started soaking the chia seeds overnight in filtered water and then adding them to my green juice the next day. Soaking chia seeds releases all their fabulous nutrients—including super-hydrating electrolyte minerals, which will make your green juice more hydrating than ever. They also give your green juice an interesting texture.

SUPERFOOD HIGHLIGHT

CHIA SEEDS

Chia seeds are a true superfood. The ancient Mayans and Aztecs of Mexico used them for energy; in fact, "chia" is the Mayan word for "strength." Packed with soluble fiber and those ultra-healthy omega-3 fats, these whole-grain seeds are also rich in protein and calcium. Chia seeds are also wonderful in ground form, which can be added to a green smoothie or sprinkled on top of a raw salad. You'll find them in dried form at your local health-food store, and when kept dry, they can be stored for long periods of time (read: years!).

INGREDIENTS

- ❋ 1 cucumber
- ❋ Big handful spinach (⅔ bunch)
- ❋ Handful fresh mint (3 or 4 leaves; optional)
- ❋ ½ cup (80 g) cantaloupe chunks
- ❋ ½ cup (80 g) watermelon chunks
- ❋ ⅛ teaspoon Himalayan pink salt
- ❋ ¼ cup (40 g) chia seeds, soaked overnight in filtered water (optional)

METHOD

1. Wash the cucumber, spinach, and mint.
2. Run all ingredients except salt and seeds through your juicer and scrape off foam (if desired).
3. Sprinkle in the salt and chia seeds (if using), stir, and enjoy!

SWEET HONEYDEW JUICE

Honeydew is one of my favorite summertime fruits. Related to watermelon and cantaloupe (but better!), it simply melts in your mouth. It sweetens up a green juice really nicely.

INGREDIENTS

❋ 1 cucumber

❋ Big handful spinach (⅔ bunch)

❋ ½ cup (75 g) green grapes

❋ ½ cup (90 g) honeydew melon chunks

METHOD

① Wash the cucumber, spinach, and grapes.

② Run all ingredients through your juicer, scrape off foam (if desired), and enjoy.

PEACH PINEAPPLE JUICE

Peaches may be my all-time favorite fruit during the summer. I love stopping at farm stands and buying them directly from farmers. Never refrigerate them, as they taste much better warm and ripe straight from the farm. They make a scrumptious addition to a green juice.

INGREDIENTS

- ❋ 1 cucumber
- ❋ 1 peach
- ❋ Big handful spinach (⅔ bunch)
- ❋ Handful fresh mint (3 or 4 leaves)
- ❋ ¼-inch (6 mm) piece ginger root
- ❋ ⅛ pineapple or 1 cup (165 g) pineapple chunks (fresh or frozen)

METHOD

1. Wash the cucumber, peach, spinach, mint, and ginger.
2. Cut and core the peach and cut into pieces that will fit through your juicer.
3. Top and tail the pineapple, peel it, and cut into pieces that will fit through your juicer.
4. Run all ingredients through your juicer, scrape off foam (if desired), and enjoy!

SUPERFOOD HIGHLIGHT

GINGER ROOT

Ginger root has been used for centuries to alleviate symptoms of gastrointestinal upset and as an aid for digestion. Recently, ginger has been shown in studies to help prevent and ease symptoms of motion sickness, including nausea, vomiting, and dizziness. It can be easily stored, unsealed, in the crisper drawer of your refrigerator for long periods of time.

ZUCCHINI PEAR JUICE

Zucchini makes a perfect substitute for cucumber in any green juice. It gives the juice a slightly creamy texture. I love using zucchini in my green juice all summer long while they are abundantly in season.

INGREDIENTS

※ 1 pear

※ 1 zucchini

※ Big handful spinach (⅔ bunch)

※ Handful fresh cilantro (coriander) leaves (from 3 or 4 stems)

METHOD

① Wash all ingredients well.

② Cut and core the pear and cut into pieces that will fit through your juicer.

③ Chop the zucchini into pieces that will fit through your juicer.

④ Run all ingredients through your juicer, scrape off foam (if desired), and enjoy!

SUPERFOOD HIGHLIGHT

CILANTRO

Some people absolutely love cilantro; others report that it tastes like soap. If you are in the "soap" category, just skip it in lieu of another dark leafy herb. However, if you are one of the lucky folks who find the smell "intoxicating," use it often in green juices or smoothies or tossed into your favorite salad. Cilantro offers loads of antioxidants, phytonutrients, and minerals such as calcium and potassium. You'll also get vitamins A, C, and K, and even some B vitamins from this potent herb. To store cilantro, loosely wrap the stems in a paper towel to keep it free of moisture. Place it in a plastic bag and store in the fridge to preserve it for a longer period of time. Stored properly, it can last up to three days. When juicing, cut off the long stems, as they can be bitter.

YELLOW BELL PEPPER JUICE

Don't let the color of this drink fool you. It's chock-full of green goodness. And if you're ready to go "fruitless," this savory recipe is just the juice for you!

INGREDIENTS

❀ 1 cucumber

❀ 3 to 5 celery ribs, bottoms removed

❀ 2 or 3 kale leaves

❀ 1 yellow bell pepper (yellow capsicum)

❀ Handful fresh basil (3 or 4 leaves)

❀ ½ lemon, peeled (optional)

METHOD

1. Wash the cucumber, celery, kale, bell pepper, and basil.

2. Remove the top and seeds from the bell pepper and cut into pieces that will fit through your juicer.

3. If you need to cut the greenness, use ½ lemon. If not, skip it.

4. Run all ingredients through your juicer, scrape off foam (if desired), and enjoy!

HONEYDEW WATERCRESS JUICE

This green juice combines three of my favorite summer ingredients: sweet honeydew, creamy zucchini, and a touch of spiciness from the watercress.

INGREDIENTS

❀ 1 zucchini

❀ Handful watercress (⅓ bunch)

❀ Handful fresh cilantro (coriander) leaves (from 3 or 4 stems)

❀ 3 or 4 celery ribs, bottoms removed

❀ 1 cup (180 g) honeydew melon chunks

❀ ⅛ tsp Himalayan pink salt (optional, but recommended)

METHOD

① Wash the zucchini, watercress, cilantro, and celery.

② Run all ingredients through your juicer and scrape off foam (if desired).

③ Season with salt, if desired, stir, and enjoy!

ZUCCHINI CANTALOUPE JUICE

Cantaloupe and zucchini actually come from the same plant family, so they combine well in a green juice. They both grow from vines that crawl across the ground. In my mom's garden, I loved hunting and picking them when growing up.

INGREDIENTS

❀ 1 zucchini

❀ Big handful spinach (⅔ bunch)

❀ Handful fresh basil (3 or 4 leaves)

❀ 1 cup (160 g) cantaloupe chunks

❀ ¼ lemon, peeled

❀ Himalayan pink salt, to taste

METHOD

① Wash the zucchini, spinach, and basil.

② Run all ingredients except salt through your juicer and scrape off foam (if desired).

③ Sprinkle in a dash of salt, stir, and enjoy!

SUPERFOOD HIGHLIGHT

SPINACH

Spinach is one of the most nutrient-dense foods in existence. A single cup is a great source of calcium and iron, and it contains far more vitamin K than the daily allowance, as well as high doses of vitamin A and magnesium. Spinach, unlike most other dark leafy greens, is actually pretty neutral from a flavor perspective. As a result, it makes a fantastic base for a green juice or green smoothie. Baby spinach is also a wonderful addition to any salad.

Do not wash spinach before storing, as the exposure to water encourages spoilage. Place spinach in a plastic storage bag and wrap the bag tightly around the spinach, squeezing out as much of the air as possible. Store in the refrigerator, where it will keep fresh for up to five days.

DANDELION GREENS JUICE

You can buy dandelion greens at your local health-food store. Never pick them from your yard! Pesticides are used abundantly on lawns, and even if you don't use pesticides on your lawn, your neighbors most likely do on theirs, and these pesticides will find their way onto the weeds. Once you get your "weeds" home, store them in an airtight bag in the refrigerator. Do not wash them before storing, as contact with water can facilitate spoilage. When you are ready to use them, simply wash well and throw them into your juicer, stems and all.

SUPERFOOD HIGHLIGHT

DANDELION GREENS

Who knew that these would be one of the best things to throw into your juicer? Dandelion greens have some powerful health benefits, as they detoxify, fight allergies, and help normalize blood sugar. Cultivated in the wild, dandelion greens are high in vitamins A, B1, B2, B6, and magnesium, and they are also packed with iron, potassium, and calcium.

INGREDIENTS

❋ 1 cucumber

❋ 3 celery ribs, bottoms removed

❋ Big handful spinach (⅔ bunch)

❋ Handful dandelion greens (5 or 6 stems)

❋ Handful fresh basil (3 or 4 leaves)

❋ ½ lemon, peeled (optional)

METHOD

① Wash the cucumber, celery, spinach, dandelion greens, and basil.

② If you need to cut the greenness, use ½ lemon. If not, skip it.

③ Run all ingredients through your juicer, scrape off foam (if desired), and enjoy!

SHAUNA'S HUNGRY GIRL (OR GUY) SANDWICH

Sometimes, a good old-fashioned sandwich really hits the spot. When making a sandwich, I always try to use whole-grain bread instead of refined bread. One favorite is the sprouted Ezekiel grain bread made by Food for Life. Because the grains are sprouted, they have more nutrients than regular grains plus additional fiber.

INGREDIENTS

- ❀ 2 slices sprouted-grain bread
- ❀ 1 tablespoon vegan mayo (such as Vegenaise by Follow Your Heart brand)
- ❀ ½ avocado, sliced
- ❀ ½ medium tomato, sliced
- ❀ 1 or 2 butter lettuce leaves
- ❀ 1 or 2 freshbasil leaves
- ❀ Handful of sprouts (any kind)

METHOD

1. Spread the sprouted-grain slices with vegan mayo.
2. Add the avocado and tomato slices.
3. Layer on the lettuce and basil leaves.
4. Add sprouts, close up the sandwich, and enjoy!

GAZPACHO

One of my favorite summer treats is freshly made raw gazpacho. I love grabbing all the ingredients from a summer farmers market and blending up a big batch to enjoy over the course of several days. It takes just seconds to prepare, and it's even better the next day—stored in an airtight container in the refrigerator overnight.

INGREDIENTS

- ❃ 1 yellow bell pepper (yellow capsicum)
- ❃ Handful fresh basil (6 or 7 leaves)
- ❃ ½ jalapeño, seeded
- ❃ 1 cucumber, peeled and cut into large chunks
- ❃ 1 sweet onion, cut into quarters
- ❃ 2 garlic cloves, peeled
- ❃ 1 cup (235 ml) water
- ❃ 2 tablespoons extra-virgin olive oil
- ❃ 2 tablespoons white vinegar
- ❃ 4 or 5 ripe tomatoes, cut in halves or quarters
- ❃ Sea salt, to taste
- ❃ Freshly ground black pepper, to taste

METHOD

1. Combine all ingredients except tomatoes in a high-speed blender or Vitamix and blend on chopped setting.
2. Add tomatoes and pulse until desired consistency.
3. Season with salt and black pepper.

VEGAN CAESAR SALAD

I love the flavor profile of Caesar salad, but I missed out on eating it for years until I figured out a substitute for the dressing.

INGREDIENTS

- ❋ 4 or 5 heart of romaine (cos) leaves, roughly chopped
- ❋ Handful fresh parsley leaves (from 5 or 6 stems), chopped
- ❋ ½ cup (75g) raw cashew nuts or pine nuts (I prefer pine nuts)
- ❋ 2 tablespoons fresh lemon juice
- ❋ ½ teaspoon raw coconut nectar
- ❋ 3 tablespoons nutritional yeast flakes
- ❋ 1 or 2 garlic cloves
- ❋ ½ teaspoon sea salt, or more to taste
- ❋ ½ teaspoon freshly ground black pepper, or more to taste

METHOD

1. Combine the romaine and parsley in a large bowl and toss.
2. To make the dressing, combine all remaining ingredients in your high-speed blender or Vitamix, and blend on High.
3. Pour the dressing over the chopped romaine and toss to mix well.

GUACAMOLE TACOS

These tacos are so fun and should hit the spot for Tex-Mex night. A Texas staple, guacamole is also a wonderful raw, vegan dip. It works perfectly as the base for a romaine lettuce wrap.

INGREDIENTS

GUACAMOLE

❋ 2 avocados, chopped

❋ 2 roma tomatoes, chopped

❋ ¼ red onion, finely chopped

❋ 1 or 2 garlic cloves, finely chopped

❋ ½ jalapeño, seeds removed and finely chopped

❋ ½ bunch fresh cilantro (coriander), leaves only, chopped

❋ Juice of ½ lime

❋ Sea salt, to taste

❋ Freshly ground black pepper, to taste

❋ Dash cayenne pepper (optional)

TACOS

❋ 4 or 5 heart of romaine (cos) leaves

❋ 2 to 3 tablespoons raw pumpkin seeds

❋ 1 cup (50 g) sprouts (any kind)

METHOD

1. Combine avocado, tomatoes, onion, garlic, and jalapeño in a small bowl. Stir with a fork until the avocado is chunky.

2. Add the cilantro and lime juice, then season with salt and black pepper to taste.

3. If you like spice, add a dash of cayenne and mix well into the guacamole.

4. Arrange the romaine leaves on a plate and add a scoop of guacamole on each leaf. Top with pumpkin seeds and sprouts.

5. To eat, fold up the sides of the leaf like a taco, and enjoy.

SUMMER GRILLED SALAD

During the summer, my friends and family are usually grilling all forms of meat, especially burgers and hot dogs. Not wanting to miss out on the fun, I decided to come up with my own grilled plant-based dish.

INGREDIENTS

- ❀ I head romaine (cos) lettuce
- ❀ I head radicchio
- ❀ 3 tablespoons extra-virgin olive oil, plus more for brushing
- ❀ Sea salt, to taste
- ❀ Freshly ground black pepper, to taste
- ❀ I package (roll) polenta
- ❀ I tablespoon raw apple cider vinegar (I recommend Bragg's)
- ❀ I tablespoon whole-grain mustard
- ❀ I green onion, thinly sliced

METHOD

1. Prep the grill to normal grilling temperature.

2. Separate the romaine leaves and chop the head of radicchio in half. Brush each leaf and each radicchio half with olive oil and sprinkle with salt and black pepper.

3. Slice the roll of polenta lengthwise into three or four slices that are each about I inch (2.5 cm) thick. Brush the polenta slices with olive oil and sprinkle with salt and black pepper.

4. To prepare the dip or dressing for the grilled vegetables, combine 3 tablespoons of olive oil with the apple cider vinegar, mustard, and green onion, and whisk until well mixed.

5. Grill the lettuce and polenta, taking care not to burn them. The lettuce should just be wilted in order to get a grilled flavor.

6. Roughly chop the grilled romaine, radicchio, and polenta, and combine on a plate or serving platter.

7. Pour the dressing over the salad and toss, or use as a dip.

SUMMER QUINOA SALAD

Quinoa is a wonderful grain that is high in protein. As a result, it is a wonderful addition to a plant-based diet and is far superior to other grains, which do not contain very much protein. This salad makes a fantastic summer treat using colorful summer vegetables from the farmers market.

INGREDIENTS

- ❈ 1 cup (170 g) quinoa
- ❈ 1 medium carrot, shredded or diced, or ½ cup (60 g) shredded carrot
- ❈ ½ red pepper (red capsicum), finely diced
- ❈ ½ yellow pepper (yellow capsicum), finely diced
- ❈ ½ cup (35 g) green cabbage, shredded
- ❈ ½ cup (35 g) red cabbage, shredded
- ❈ Handful fresh cilantro (coriander) leaves (from 5 or 6 stems), torn into pieces
- ❈ Handful fresh basil (6 or 7 leaves), torn into pieces
- ❈ 2 tablespoons sesame oil
- ❈ 1 tablespoon raw coconut vinegar or rice vinegar
- ❈ ½-inch (13 mm) piece ginger root, minced
- ❈ 1 tablespoon black sesame seeds

METHOD

1. Rinse and boil the quinoa for about 15 minutes, or until soft (or follow instructions on package). Transfer to a large bowl.

2. Combine all vegetables and herbs with the quinoa and toss well.

3. To make the dressing, whisk together the sesame oil, vinegar, ginger, and sesame seeds.

4. Pour the dressing over the quinoa-vegetable mix and toss gently until everything is coated.

Fall

The wonderful flavors of fall make this season an incredible time to juice. Plus, fall juicing is a fantastic way to get healthy and focused before the upcoming holiday season. Here's a convenient shopping list for making all eleven of the energizing superfood smoothies and juices in this section.

JUICE SHOPPING LIST

VEGETABLES	QUANTITY
BROCCOLI	½ stalk (florets removed)
CARROTS	2 medium
CELERY	3 heads
CUCUMBERS	4 medium
FENNEL	1 bulb
GINGER	½-inch (13mm) piece
KALE	3 bunches
JALAPEÑO	1 small
RED BELL PEPPER (RED CAPSICUM)	1 medium
ROMAINE (COS)	1 head
SPINACH	2 bunches or 1 large box, pre-washed
ZUCCHINI	1 medium

FRUIT	QUANTITY
APPLES	2 medium
AVOCADO	1 small
GRANNY SMITH APPLE	1 medium
GREEN GRAPES	1 bunch
LEMONS	2 medium
ORANGE	1 medium
PINEAPPLE	1 whole

HERBS	QUANTITY
BASIL	1 bunch
CILANTRO (CORIANDER)	1 bunch
PARSLEY	1 bunch

OTHER	QUANTITY
CAYENNE PEPPER	small amount
GROUND CINNAMON (OPTIONAL)	small amount
SALT (HIMALAYAN PINK)	1 shaker of whole crystals
TURMERIC POWDER	small amount
VANILLA EXTRACT (PURE)	1 small vile

FALL MORNING GREEN JUICE

My favorite part of the morning: preparing my morning green juice. As you can probably tell by now, I have a serious love affair with my morning green juice. Now it is time to start your own love affair!

INGREDIENTS

❁ 5 or 6 celery ribs, bottoms removed

❁ 4 or 5 kale leaves

❁ 1 apple

❁ Handful fresh parsley leaves (from 3 or 4 stems)

METHOD

① Wash the celery, kale, apple, and parsley.

② Cut and core the apple and cut into pieces that will fit through your juicer.

③ Run all ingredients through your juicer, scrape off foam (if desired), and enjoy!

CREAMY AVOCADO
SMOOTHIE

Avocados get a bad wrap for being high in calories and fat; however, these are the good kinds of fats—the ones that help lower your cholesterol. Even better? Avocado makes a smoothie creamy, filling, and delicious.

INGREDIENTS

- ❀ Big handful spinach (⅔ bunch)
- ❀ 1 small avocado or ½ large avocado
- ❀ ½ banana (fresh or frozen)
- ❀ 1 cup (235 ml) filtered water (or coconut water if desired)
- ❀ 1 teaspoon pure vanilla extract
- ❀ Dash cinnamon (optional)

METHOD

① Wash the spinach.

② Remove the flesh from the avocado.

③ Add all ingredients to your high-speed blender or Vitamix, and blend on High until smooth and creamy.

④ Add more water if needed to obtain desired consistency for drinking.

SPICY PINEAPPLE
GINGER SMOOTHIE

This smoothie is nice and green, but has a fun spicy kick to it because of the ginger and cayenne. It will definitely wake up your taste buds first thing in the morning.

INGREDIENTS

- ⚜ 3 or 4 kale leaves
- ⚜ Handful fresh cilantro (coriander) leaves (from 3 or 4 stems)
- ⚜ ¼-inch (6 mm) piece ginger root
- ⚜ 1 cup (165 g) pineapple chunks (fresh or frozen)
- ⚜ ½ cup (120 ml) filtered water
- ⚜ Pinch cayenne pepper

METHOD

1. Wash the kale, cilantro, and ginger root.
2. Add all ingredients to your high-speed blender or Vitamix, and blend on High until smooth and creamy.
3. Add more water if needed to obtain desired consistency for drinking.

PINEAPPLE GREEN JUICE

If you're not yet on board with the taste of green juice, this is a great beginner green juice. It doesn't contain any dark leafy greens, so it technically does not follow the "Simple Green Juice Formula." However, it's a terrific way to ease into green juice.

INGREDIENTS

- 1 cucumber
- 4 or 5 celery ribs, bottoms removed
- 2 or 3 romaine (cos) leaves
- ¼ pineapple or 1½ cups (250 g) pineapple chunks (fresh or frozen)
- ¼ lemon, peeled

METHOD

1. Wash the cucumber, celery, and romaine.
2. Top and tail the pineapple, peel it, and cut into pieces that will fit through your juicer.
3. Run all ingredients through your juicer, scrape off foam (if desired), and enjoy!

ZUCCHINI APPLE JUICE

Zucchini is a wonderful substitute for cucumber in a green juice, and it adds a nice creamy texture. While it is technically a summer vegetable, it usually peaks late in the season and can often be found at early-fall farmers markets.

INGREDIENTS

- 1 zucchini
- 4 or 5 kale leaves
- 1 Granny Smith apple
- ¼ lemon, peeled

METHOD

1. Wash the zucchini, kale, and apple.
2. Cut and core the apple and cut into pieces that will fit through the juicer.
3. Run all ingredients through your juicer, scrape off foam (if desired), and enjoy!

APPLE FENNEL JUICE

Fennel is one of my favorite ingredients to add to both salads and green juice. Although related to carrots, dill, parsley, and cilantro, fennel has a distinct taste (kind of like licorice) that adds a big punch of flavor to your juice.

INGREDIENTS

- 4 or 5 celery ribs, bottoms removed
- 4 or 5 kale leaves
- 1 apple
- ¼ fennel bulb
- ¼ lemon, peeled

METHOD

1. Wash the celery, kale, apple, and fennel.
2. Cut and core the apple and cut into pieces that will fit through your juicer.
3. Run all ingredients through your juicer, scrape off foam (if desired), and enjoy.

SUPERFOOD HIGHLIGHT

FENNEL

Fennel is rich in vitamin C, which helps boost the immune system, and it also contains potassium, calcium, iron, manganese, copper, phosphorus, and folate. Another bonus? You can eat the whole vegetable, from its white or light-green bulb to its stalks and fluffy green fronds. I tend to use the bulb for salads and the whole thing for juicing. Fennel is in season from fall through spring and can be found at your local natural-food store. When shopping for fennel, look for bulbs that are clean, firm, and solid. Store fresh fennel in your refrigerator's crisper, where it should keep fresh for about four days.

ORANGE CARROT PINEAPPLE JUICE

Though I really believe in the power of drinking your greens, drinking your carrots is equally beneficial. I had so many requests for a carrot juice that I set out to create one.

INGREDIENTS

- 2 medium carrots, tops and bottoms removed
- 1 cucumber
- Small handful spinach (½ bunch)
- ⅛ pineapple or 1 cup (165 g) pineapple chunks (fresh or frozen)
- ½ orange, peeled
- ¼ lemon, peeled
- Dash turmeric powder (½ teaspoon or less)

METHOD

(1) Wash the carrots, cucumber, and spinach.

(2) Top and tail the pineapple, peel it, and cut into pieces that will fit through your juicer.

(3) Run all ingredients except turmeric through your juicer and scrape off foam (if desired).

(4) Add turmeric, stir, and enjoy!

GRAPE GINGER JUICE

Kale serves as an amazing base for a green juice or green smoothie, and baby kale leaves make a wonderful addition to any salad. When shopping for kale, you might see a few different varieties, including curly kale, ornamental kale, and dinosaur kale. You can use them all for juicing, but I recommend dinosaur kale, as it usually results in the most juice.

INGREDIENTS

- ⚜ 1 cup (150 g) green grapes
- ⚜ 5 or 6 kale leaves
- ⚜ 2 or 3 romaine (cos) leaves
- ⚜ ¼-inch (6 mm) piece ginger root
- ⚜ ¼ lemon, peeled

METHOD

1. Wash the grapes, kale, romaine, and ginger.
2. Run all ingredients through your juicer, scrape off foam (if desired), and enjoy!

SUPERFOOD HIGHLIGHT

KALE

Kale contains high quantities of powerful antioxidants, such as vitamins A and C, and it's loaded with vitamin K. It's a good source of vitamins B1, B2, and B6, as well as the all-important electrolyte minerals sodium, potassium, calcium, and magnesium. It's also a detoxing dynamo, helping the body to clear out toxins. Store your kale in an airtight plastic bag in the refrigerator for up to five days. Don't wash kale before storing. When you're ready for juicing, simply wash and use the entire leaf. However, if you're making a delicate salad, use only the leaves and either discard the stems or save them for juicing.

PINEAPPLE JALAPEÑO JUICE

Jalapeños have many fantastic nutrients, including high doses of vitamin C. In fact, one small jalapeño provides a day's worth of vitamin C. Adding a bit of jalapeño to a green juice really mixes things up and adds a fun new dimension.

INGREDIENTS

- ½ cucumber
- 3 or 4 celery ribs, bottoms removed
- 4 or 5 kale leaves
- ¼ jalapeño or more if desired, seeded (optional, but recommended)
- ⅛ pineapple or 1 cup (165 g) pineapple chunks (fresh or frozen)
- ⅛ teaspoon Himalyayan pink salt (optional, but recommended)

METHOD

1. Wash the cucumber, celery, kale and jalapeño.
2. Top and tail the pineapple, peel it, and cut into pieces that will fit through your juicer.
3. Run all ingredients except jalapeño through your juicer.
4. Add 1/4 portion of jalapeño and taste to check spice level. If more spice is needed, add more jalapeño a little at a time until the desired spiciness is obtained.
5. Scrape off foam and sprinkle with salt (if desired), stir, and enjoy!

RED BELL PEPPER JUICE

Red peppers (red capsicum) are not only full of vitamin C and other antioxidants, they also have a wonderful sweetness that is a great substitute for fruit in a green juice.

INGREDIENTS

- 3 to 5 celery ribs, bottoms removed
- Big handful spinach (⅔ bunch)
- 2 or 3 romaine (cos) leaves
- I red bell pepper (red capsicum)
- Handful fresh parsley leaves (from 3 or 4 stems)
- ¼ lemon, peeled (optional)

METHOD

1. Wash the celery, spinach, romaine, bell pepper, and parsley.
2. Remove the top and seeds from the bell pepper and cut into pieces that will fit through your juicer.
3. If you need to cut the greenness, use ¼ lemon. If not, skip it.
4. Run all ingredients through your juicer, scrape off foam (if desired), and enjoy!

BROCCOLI BASIL JUICE

When my son, Cooper, was young, I used to steam broccoli for him and he would only eat the tops—or the "trees," as he called them. Trying to find a use for the remaining broccoli stalks, one day I threw a stalk in the juicer with my morning green juice. I was hooked.

INGREDIENTS

- 1 cucumber
- 3 celery ribs, bottoms removed
- 3 or 4 kale leaves
- ½ stalk broccoli (no floret)
- Handful fresh basil (6 or 7 leaves)
- ½ lemon, peeled (optional)

METHOD

1. Wash the cucumber, celery, kale, broccoli, and basil.
2. If you need to cut the greenness, use ½ lemon. If not, skip it.
3. Run all ingredients through your juicer, scrape off foam (if desired), and enjoy!

SUPERFOOD HIGHLIGHT

BROCCOLI

With an impressive lineup of nutrients, including high quantities of vitamins A and C, broccoli is also packed with potassium, calcium, and iron. Researchers are constantly studying the wonderful cancer-fighting qualities of broccoli, along with its unique ability to help lower cholesterol. Broccoli also contains the all-important vitamin D, a vitamin in which many people are deficient. To store, place broccoli in a plastic bag, removing as much of the air from the bag as possible. Broccoli will stay fresh in the refrigerator for up to ten days, but be sure to store it dry.

ACORN SQUASH
AND WHEATBERRY SALAD

Wheatberries are the hard kernels from the wheat plant. They are the whole grain, containing the bran, germ, and endosperm. Because they are not refined in anyway and are a great source of fiber, I love combining them with fall vegetables for a filling fall meal. Wheatberries need to soak overnight, so keep that in mind if you're going to make this delicious salad.

INGREDIENTS

- 🍁 1 cup (180 g) raw wheatberries, soaked overnight
- 🍁 1 acorn squash (or butternut squash), peeled and cubed
- 🍁 3 tablespoons extra-virgin olive oil, divided
- 🍁 Sea salt, to taste
- 🍁 Freshly ground black pepper, to taste
- 🍁 1 tablespoon raw whole-grain mustard
- 🍁 1 tablespoon maple syrup
- 🍁 1 teaspoon lemon juice
- 🍁 ¼ cup (40 g) dried cranberries
- 🍁 ½ bag baby spinach or arugula (rocket; or combination of both)

METHOD

1. Boil the wheatberries until soft and edible. This can take up to 30 minutes.
2. Preheat the oven to 425°F (220°C).
3. Combine the acorn squash with 1 tablespoon of the olive oil and salt and black pepper to taste.
4. Transfer to a baking dish or baking sheet and cover with foil. Bake for 30 minutes, or until squash is soft. To check for doneness, insert a knife into a squash cube.
5. To make the dressing, whisk together the remaining 2 tablespoons olive oil, mustard, maple syrup, and lemon juice in a small bowl.
6. When the wheatberries are done, drain and transfer to a salad bowl.
7. Pour the dressing over the wheatberries and toss to coat.
8. Add the squash and cranberries and toss gently.
9. Add the spinach or arugula and toss gently to combine. Serve hot or cold.

RAW BUTTERNUT SQUASH SOUP

Time for some delicious raw soup! This recipe is a raw version of my favorite holiday vegetable dish that I prepare for both Thanksgiving and Christmas. The cooked version involves a baked butternut squash garnished with dried or fresh cranberries and wilted garlic spinach. It is such a hit during the holidays that I was determined to recreate these wonderful flavors in the form of a raw soup. If you need a little warmth, you can heat the soup a bit on the stove without cooking away all the nutrients. The raw food temperature limit is 115°F (50°C). When your food spends any time above this temperature, it will start to lose nutrients at a rapid rate.

INGREDIENTS

- ½ small butternut squash, peeled and cubed
- ½ medium avocado or 1 small avocado
- 1 cup (235 ml) filtered water
- 1 tablespoon extra-virgin olive oil
- 2 tablespoons maple syrup
- 1 garlic clove, peeled
- Sea salt, to taste
- Freshly ground black pepper, to taste
- Handful dried cranberries (for garnish)

METHOD

1. Combine the butternut squash, avocado flesh, water, olive oil, maple syrup, and garlic in a high-speed blender or Vitamix.

2. Blend on High until smooth, adding more water as needed until it reaches desired consistency. Season with salt and black pepper.

3. If you would like a warm soup while keeping it raw, pour it into a saucepan on the stove and heat over the lowest possible temperature. Stir constantly until the soup is warm to the touch. Remove immediately. Ladle into a bowl and garnish with pepper and dried cranberries.

RAW CARROT SOUP

When I step into fall, I always get the urge to make soup; however, most soups cook down vegetables to the point where there are not many nutrients left. So, I learned about raw soups many years ago and became hooked. If you need a little warmth, you can heat the soup a bit on the stove without cooking away all the nutrients. The raw food temperature limit is 115°F (50°C). When your food spends any time above this temperature, it will start to lose nutrients at a rapid rate.

INGREDIENTS

- ❀ 2 medium carrots, roughly chopped
- ❀ ½ red bell pepper (red capsicum), seeded and roughly chopped
- ❀ ¼-inch (6 mm) piece ginger root
- ❀ Handful fresh parsley leaves (from 5 or 6 stems)
- ❀ 1 avocado
- ❀ ½ to 1 cup (120 to 235 ml) water
- ❀ Sea salt, to taste
- ❀ Freshly ground black pepper, to taste
- ❀ Extra-virgin olive oil, for drizzling

METHOD

1. Wash the carrots, bell pepper, ginger, and parsley.
2. Place the carrots, bell pepper, ginger, half of parsley, and avocado flesh in a high-speed blender or Vitamix.
3. Blend on High until smooth, adding water as needed until it reaches desired consistency. Season with salt and black pepper.
4. If you would like a warm soup while keeping it raw, pour it into a saucepan on the stove and heat over the lowest possible temperature. Stir constantly until the soup is warm to the touch. Remove immediately.
5. Ladle into a bowl, drizzle with olive oil, and garnish with remaining parsley leaves.

FALL FENNEL SALAD

This is one of my favorite salads as the summer fades into cooler weather. I have been making this salad for years for my friends and family, and I seem to make it a bit differently each time depending on what herbs and nuts I have on hand. The taste can change dramatically if you alter the combinations, so feel free to experiment and find the perfect blend of herbs and nuts for your version.

INGREDIENTS

- Large bowl of baby mixed greens (such as baby red and green romaine [cos])
- ½ fennel bulb, finely sliced
- ½ cup (75 g) cherry tomatoes, halved
- Handful fresh tarragon (from 2 or 3 stems), finely chopped
- Handful fresh basil (6 or 7 leaves), finely chopped
- ¼ cup (35 g) pine nuts
- 2 teaspoons fresh lemon juice (juice of ½ lemon)
- 2 teaspoons almond oil
- Sea salt, to taste
- Freshly ground black pepper, to taste
- ½ avocado or 1 small avocado, thinly sliced

METHOD

1. Gently toss together the mixed greens, fennel, tomatoes, tarragon, and basil in a large bowl.
2. Add the pine nuts, lemon juice, and almond oil, and toss to combine. Season with salt and black pepper.
3. Layer the sliced avocado over the top of the salad, and enjoy!

AUTUMN BUTTERNUT SQUASH WITH SPINACH

I came up with this dish for our annual Halloween potluck gathering at a dear friend's house. Her husband is a chef and other chef friends attend, so I wanted to bring something special. This dish has become such a hit that I usually make it for Thanksgiving and Christmas holiday potlucks as well. I have sized this recipe down to make a hearty dinner for one.

INGREDIENTS

- ½ butternut squash, seeded
- 3 tablespoons extra-virgin olive oil, divided
- 1 tablespoon pure maple syrup
- 2 tablespoons dried cranberries
- 2 tablespoons pine nuts
- 1 bunch spinach, stems removed, or 1 bag baby spinach
- 2 or 3 garlic cloves, minced

METHOD

1. Preheat the oven to 425°F (220°C).
2. Place the squash half into a small glass casserole dish and add 1 tablespoon of olive oil and the maple syrup into the center hole of the squash.
3. Cover with foil and bake for 45 minutes, or until squash is soft (check for doneness by inserting a knife into thickest portion of squash to make sure it is soft all the way through).
4. Meanwhile, in a medium nonstick skillet, sauté the cranberries and pine nuts in 1 tablespoon of olive oil until the pine nuts are brown. Remove and set aside.
5. Heat the remaining1 tablespoon olive oil in the same skillet. Add the minced garlic and sauté for 1 minute, or until brown.
6. Add the spinach and sauté for 2 to 3 minutes, mixing with the garlic, until the spinach is wilted but not cooked.
7. To serve, place the butternut squash on a plate or serving platter and arrange the wilted spinach around the outside. Sprinkle the squash with pine nuts and cranberries, and enjoy!

HEAVENLY HERB SALAD

This salad is one of my all-time favorites—it's like a comfort food. The mixture of avocado and almonds makes it hearty and filling. But for me, the essence of a salad is in its herbs, and this one has three of my favorites: mint, basil, and cilantro. One of my dear chef friends, John Cain, requests that I make this salad for him frequently. It is so fun to watch him eat it, as he makes cute happy noises the entire time. I think that he too is completely seduced by the heavenly combination of herbs.

INGREDIENTS

- Large bowl of baby mixed greens (such as red and green romaine [cos])
- Handful fresh mint (6 or 7 leaves), finely chopped
- Handful fresh basil (6 or 7 leaves), finely chopped
- Handful fresh cilantro (coriander) leaves (from 5 or 6 stems), finely chopped
- 1 small avocado or ½ large avocado, diced
- 1 tablespoon dried currants
- 1 tablespoon roughly chopped almonds
- 1 tablespoon almond oil
- 1 teaspoon agave nectar
- Juice of ½ lime
- Sea salt, to taste

METHOD

1. Toss together the mixed greens, mint, basil, and cilantro in a large bowl.
2. Add the avocado, currants, almonds, almond oil, agave nectar, and lime juice, and toss again.
3. Season with salt, and enjoy!

CRUNCHY ROSEMARY SALAD

Living in Texas, I have rosemary that grows like a weed year-round in my front yard. Since this is the only herb that I seem to be able to grow in this climate, I decided to incorporate it into a salad. While it is certainly an unusual ingredient for a salad, I think it adds a really fun taste and texture. Just make sure to chop it very finely and avoid overdoing it.

INGREDIENTS

- Large bowl of baby mixed greens (such as red and green romaine [cos])
- Handful fresh tarragon leaves (from 2 or 3 stems) finely chopped
- Handful of fresh leaves (from 1 or 2 stems), finely chopped
- Juice of ½ lime
- 2 tablespoons hemp seeds
- 2 tablespoons almond oil
- Sea salt, to taste
- 4 or 5 raw crackers, broken into pieces (I like Two Moms in the Raw brand)
- 1 avocado, thinly sliced

METHOD

1. Toss together the mixed greens, tarragon, and rosemary in a large bowl.
2. Add the lime juice, hemp seeds, and almond oil, and toss again.
3. Season with salt, add crackers, and toss once more.
4. Arrange a layer of avocado slices over the top, and enjoy!

INDEX

Page references in *italics* indicate images.

Acknowledgments

Thank you to Mayim Bialik for being such a wonderful supporter and to Lauren Minchen for all that you do for Daily Greens.

Thank you to the entire Daily Greens team. You all inspire me each and every day!

Finally, thank you to my ever-supportive husband, Kirk, and my beautiful son, Cooper. You are my sunshine, my reason for being, my everything!

About the Author

Shauna R. Martin is CEO and founder of Daily Greens, a raw, cold-pressed green juice company based in Austin, Texas. In 2005, Shauna was diagnosed with breast cancer. With a young family to care for, she turned to daily green juicing to recover from the trauma of multiple surgeries and the toxic effects of chemotherapy. After discovering the life-restoring power of green juices, she made it her mission to get them into the hands of everyone that she could, so that all can thrive as she has.

In 2012, after an eighteen-year career as a corporate attorney, Shauna founded Drink Daily Greens LLC. Dedicated to sharing the benefits of green juices with as many people as possible, Shauna devotes her time to crafting new, delicious recipes and selling her Daily Greens beverages, which are available in retail outlets nationwide.

An active advocate for breast cancer issues, Shauna has served on the board of the Breast Cancer Resource Centers of Texas for the past eight years. She is also a founding member of the Pink Ribbon Cowgirls, a social network of young breast cancer survivors, as well as a frequent speaker and chair of breast cancer fundraising awards. In furtherance of Shauna's mission, a percentage of sales of Daily Greens is granted to fund organizations that provide services to young women and underserved women battling breast cancer.

Shauna lives in Austin, Texas, drinking her veggies, with her husband, Kirk, and their son, Cooper.

About the Contributor

Mayim Hoya Bialik is best known for her roles as Blossom Russo in the early-1990s NBC television sitcom *Blossom* and as Amy Farrah Fowler on the hit CBS comedy *The Big Bang Theory*, a role for which she received four Emmy nominations.

After *Blossom*, Bialik took a break from acting to earn a BS and PhD in neuroscience from UCLA. She is the author of *Beyond the Sling* (2012), *Mayim's Vegan Table* (2014), and *Girling Up* (2017), and *Boying Up* (2019).